The Academic Library

SECOND EDITION

The Academic Library

SECOND EDITION

Peter Brophy

facet publishing

Published by
Facet Publishing
7 Ridgmount Street
London WC1E 7AE

Facet Publishing is wholly owned by CILIP: the Chartered Institute of Library and Information Professionals.

First published by Library Association Publishing 2000
This second edition 2005
Reprinted 2006

British Library Cataloguing in Publication Data
A catalogue record for this book is available from the British Library.

ISBN-13: 978-1-85604-527-8
ISBN-10: 1-85604-527-7

Typeset in 11/14pt Savoy and Alternate Gothic 2 from author's disks by Facet Publishing.
Printed and bound by MPG Books Ltd, Bodmin, Cornwall.

This book is dedicated to
the staff of the Manchester Metropolitan University Library,
with thanks for their unfailing and courteous help
to a university librarian turned library user!

Contents

Preface

The intention behind this volume is to provide an introductory textbook which covers the major issues in academic libraries at the present time. Inevitably, there is a UK emphasis to the text since the intention has been to place general academic library issues in context and to link theory to practice. The context within which academic libraries operate is of supreme importance, and for this reason the book begins by examining the history, and in particular recent policy directions, of higher education. As services, academic libraries need to support the policies and practices of their institutions, and it follows that an understanding of higher education's direction is essential to any consideration of the academic library.

Libraries also operate in the broad context of global information services and increasingly information and communications technologies form the backdrop to this sector. In the UK, as in many other countries, libraries have been prominent in exploiting the opportunities that technology offers. However, operating in this complex and ever-changing arena presents a series of challenges to academic librarians, who have to continue to provide their bedrock services while investing in the new. The balance between print and electronic, between holdings and access, between providing a service and enabling a learning opportunity – all require careful planning and commitment. Achieving the optimum levels of service to the increasingly heterogeneous user populations which academic libraries serve is a major challenge. By examining different aspects of service and then looking at the ways in which an integrated whole can be developed and managed, the book tries to provide an overview of the issues which need to be considered and the context in which they occur.

In a final chapter, consideration turns to the uncertainties of the future. It is suggested that the future academic library has to be created, and that a variety of threats to the existence of libraries will have to be negotiated.

To realize this goal needs both a vision of that future and systematic attention to its achievement.

The second edition of this book has been extensively revised and a new chapter, on performance measurement, added. In the four years since its first publication there have been a significant number of developments in academic libraries while the environment in which they operate has produced new challenges as learning and research practices evolve in their use of new technologies. The higher and further education landscapes have evolved, with new legislation and significant changes to the relationships between institutions and their students. A research assessment exercise has come and gone, leaving in its wake pressures to further concentrate research in centres of international excellence. New opportunities are opening up for the academic library, but so too are threats, not least from global information services. These are exciting times!

As a former university librarian and head of a converged library and computing service, I am very much aware of the debt of gratitude I owe to very many people who have helped me to come to some understanding of what it means to manage academic libraries. Having changed career to become an academic myself, I have also become acutely aware of the service issues from the perspective of the library user. Being involved as a researcher in digital library and other research projects has helped me to understand a little of the complexities faced by any organization seeking to create its future in the networked information world. In all of these roles I have been immensely grateful to others for their insights, and this book owes much to them, too many to mention by name. Its errors, omissions and inexactitudes are, of course, entirely my own responsibility.

Peter Brophy

1

The higher education context

Introduction

The academic library has not infrequently been described as 'the heart of a university'. The expression seems to have originated with a nineteenth century President of Harvard University, Charles William Eliot, and was used in an official report at the time of the first massive expansion of the British university system in the 1960s (Committee on Higher Education, 1963). Whether it was ever an accurate metaphor – and whether it remains an acceptable description of the library's place in the modern university – is open to debate, but it illustrates the remarkably high regard in which libraries have been held by those who work and study in universities. Although university librarians have to fight hard for the resources they need to deliver services to ever increasing numbers of users in an ever more complex information-rich world, they can usually rely on the support of academic colleagues and student bodies for the concept of a 'well-found' library. Turning those benevolent sentiments into appropriate, efficient and effective services is an enormous challenge, and much of this book is concerned with how – at the start of a new millennium – that can be achieved.

One of the most important principles, when exploring the history and current state of academic libraries, is a recognition that the library is entirely dependent upon its parent institution. Although a few academic libraries, such as those of the Universities of Cambridge and Oxford (together known as 'Oxbridge'), have a national and international role which extends beyond their universities, it nevertheless remains true that the character of each library, and the types of service it emphasizes, are based upon the needs of a particular, well-defined group of users. It is not surprising, therefore, that the university library reflects its university. The same is true of libraries in colleges and, for that matter, in schools. At the simplest level, these dependencies will be seen in the subject strengths which the library displays, reflecting the teaching and research strengths of the parent institution. But more subtly, and perhaps more importantly, the nature and style of the library will reflect those of the institution. In an ancient university there may be greater emphasis on formal procedures and tradition; in a young college rapid change and responsiveness may be the order of the day in both institution and library.

In order to understand why university, and other academic libraries, are what they are today it is useful to review their development over the past decades and centuries. Universities do not spring up overnight, and the creation of a major university library service is equally dependent on a historical base. In this chapter institutional history will be explored. In Chapter 2 we will look at the development of academic libraries themselves.

The development of academic institutions: a brief overview

A moment's thought will reveal the enormous range and diversity of academic institutions which exists today. Even in one country, the UK, we can find:

- ancient universities, like Cambridge, Oxford, St Andrews and Aberdeen
- Victorian institutions associated with great industrial cities, like Leeds, Manchester, Sheffield and Bristol
- modern universities, created in the 1950s and 1960s, often on 'green field' sites, like Lancaster, York, Sussex and Stirling
- universities based on former technical, education, art and design and similar colleges, often tracing their history back to the early 19th century, like Manchester Metropolitan, Nottingham Trent, Northumbria and Glasgow Caledonian
- the Open University, a unique distance learning institution with students scattered across the UK and across the world
- specialist institutions with a narrow focus but excellence in their field, like the Central School of Speech and Drama, the Cumbria Institute of the Arts or Rose Bruford College, and the colleges of agriculture which have developed from rural county institutions
- former teacher training colleges, which have expanded their portfolios to include a wide range of generally arts and humanities-based courses, like Edge Hill at Ormskirk and St Martin's in Lancaster

- colleges of further education, found in every major town and city and providing a vast range of courses from initial academic to advanced technical qualifications
- private institutions, ranging from the University of Buckingham to myriad language training centres
- industrial and commercial education and training centres, including in-house 'universities'. The most interesting current development of this kind is the National Health Service (NHS) University, designed to offer personal and professional development opportunities to everyone working in the Service.

In this chapter, we will sketch the history of the major types of institution and examine how those histories have influenced the types of institution which we see today.

The ancient universities

A thousand years ago there were no universities. The oldest of today's universities are medieval in origin, Paris - the first - Oxford, Salerno and Bologna being founded towards the end of the 12th century. By 1500 Europe had about 75, although many were very small. In essence these were vocational institutions for the professions - the church, medicine and the law in particular. They secured an independence, under royal or papal charters, which was jealously guarded. Perkin (1984) has pointed out that what distinguished the medieval universities was 'firstly, that the lucrative professional disciplines that became the postgraduate faculties of theology, law and medicine were all taught side by side . . . second, that these advanced professional courses were preceded by a common curriculum in the seven liberal arts'. (These were grammar, logic, rhetoric, arithmetic, geometry, astronomy and music.) Teaching in these universities was essentially through lectures, discussion and debate, with the teacher guiding pupils and dissecting their arguments, a system which befitted the primarily oral culture of the day. This goes some way to explaining why the library was not pre-eminent in the university - the other explanation being the sheer rarity and cost of books.

The ancient universities of the United Kingdom - Oxford and Cambridge in England, St Andrews, Glasgow, Aberdeen and Edinburgh in

Scotland – developed slowly through the medieval period, sometimes advancing, sometimes in decline. They were greatly influenced by the Reformation, although Continental universities were more active participants and provided more of its intellectual underpinning. Nevertheless the ideas of the Reformation, and its questioning of first ecclesiastical and then government authority, brought universities into conflict with both church and state. However, universities remained small and their influence remained limited – even the English Civil War did not affect them as much as might with hindsight have been expected. During the 18th century they were effectively in decline, educating small numbers and most of those chosen by their means rather than their intellect. It was only in the 19th century that English and Scottish universities started to create truly national higher education systems and to gain international repute. While for much of that period English universities were not particularly notable for their influence and innovation, Scottish institutions had a more profound international influence and are generally recognized as the cradle of many new disciplines such as modern physical and social sciences.

University expansion in the 19th century

In the 19th century, the number of universities expanded and they started to throw off their traditional curricula. In 1826 University College London (UCL) was founded as a reaction to the exclusivity and hidebound practices of the existing universities, becoming branded by the Anglican Church as the 'Godless Institution of Gower Street' and by the Tory Press as 'The Cockney College'. King's College London was set up two years later at the instigation of the Church in an attempt to redress the balance. Interestingly, the teaching methods adopted at UCL were modelled on those of Scotland and Germany, where lectures and examinations were the norm, rather than on those of Oxbridge.

Over the next 100 years 12 'civic' universities were founded in major cities such as Leeds, Liverpool, Bristol and Manchester. They began as 'university colleges' and became autonomous, with their own royal charters, only after serving a long apprenticeship. Many received endowments from wealthy businessmen who saw the establishment of a university in 'their' city as a symbol of its success. This was a period when state funding for universities increased significantly. In 1919 the University Grants Committee

(UGC) was established to distribute Treasury grants to institutions, although the institutions themselves remained autonomous. The UGC was in many ways a curious body, since it tried - for many years successfully - to act as a buffer between government and universities, allowing the latter to receive grants with little real accountability for how the funding was spent. By 1945 67% of university income was from the UGC, yet autonomy was guarded as jealously as ever. It was to be the 1980s before this state of affairs was finally ended.

Popular education: the development of the mechanics' institutes

As early as the 1820s, concern was being expressed about the lack of education for working people in the vastly expanded industrial towns of the UK, and a movement began to found institutions which would address this problem. The first Mechanics' Institute was founded in Glasgow in 1823, and the movement spread rapidly. A typical example would be the delightfully named Preston Institution for the Diffusion of Knowledge, established in 1826. This foundation began with two elements: a lecture series and a library. Indeed, the first employee of the institution was the librarian, and in those days he was paid on the basis of a proportion of the membership fees he was able to collect!

The mechanics' institutes spread throughout the UK, especially in northern England, until by 1850 there were over 600. However, their impact on working people was limited, partly because of widespread illiteracy - a library was of little use to those who could not read - and partly because even their modest subscriptions were beyond the means (and inclination) of poor working families. However, over the years they evolved into something akin to modern technical colleges, with the emphasis on technician-level and practical skills. Some of them expanded to achieve significant regional status (Preston's, for example, becoming the renowned Harris College), taking a leading role in the training of apprentices and other skilled scientific and technical professionals. Their libraries declined under the influence of the public library movement, which was expanding rapidly following the Public Library Acts of 1850 and 1855. However, the technical colleges provided a route through which the institute libraries could develop, and where this happened it is possible to trace this heritage in many new universities' libraries. By the 1950s the former mechanics' institutes, joined by many other colleges with later foundations, formed a major sector of non-school, technician-level education although their significant contribution to the opening up of higher education was still to become apparent.

The Robbins Report and the 'new universities'

By 1963 there were 24 universities in the UK, with a total of 120,000 students, 15% of whom were at Oxford or Cambridge. The system remained the preserve of an élite, drawing almost exclusively from public and grammar schools - predominantly from the former. It was a system that had served the UK in the time of Empire, but its relevance and suitability for an age of technological progress in which the UK was but one state seeking to earn its living in an increasingly competitive world were starting to be questioned. The Robbins Committee was set up to address these issues.

Robbins recommended massive expansion: the beginning of the end of higher education for the élite and the start of 'mass higher education'. The principle on which Robbins based its recommendations became a bedrock of approaches to higher education in succeeding years: 'higher education opportunities should be available to all those who are qualified by ability and attainment to pursue them and who wish to do so'. The purposes of higher education were defined as instruction in skills, the promotion of the general powers of the mind, the advancement of learning and the transmission of a common culture and common standards of citizenship.

As a result of the Robbins Report, the colleges of advanced technology (CATs) - the successor institutions to the mechanics' institutes and similar foundations - became universities. These included the Universities of Strathclyde in Glasgow, City in London and Salford in Greater Manchester. Wholly new universities were created, usually on 'green field' sites outside cities: these included York, Lancaster, Stirling and Sussex. The result of these measures was a massive expansion of student numbers and, perhaps more important than anything else, the creation of a national system of higher education. University accounts became open to Parliamentary scrutiny, and the beginnings of a system of public accountability emerged.

The Open University

The establishment of the Open University (OU) marked a far-sighted decision by the then Labour Government to deliver higher education away from traditional campuses. Created in the face of considerable opposition, not least from established universities, the OU was truly innovative. It would use a combination of television, printed course materials, summer schools and local tutors to reach sections of the population who were excluded from traditional higher education. In particular it was designed to reach mature students who had not taken the traditional direct route from school to university. Although universities had for many years offered extra-mural (literally, 'beyond the walls') classes, these usually consisted of lectures by experts to interested audiences in village halls or the equivalent, and certainly would not lead to a degree or other qualification.

The OU set out to show that by using a combination of new and old technologies, and by drawing on the expertise of tutors in each region, it could deliver an educational experience which was equivalent to but different from the traditional on-campus course. It was funded directly by government, through the new Department of Education and Science, rather than through the University Grants Committee. The suspicion with which traditional universities treated it is exemplified by the exclusion, for some years, of its vice-chancellor from the Committee of Vice-Chancellors and Principals. Yet it quickly achieved remarkable growth and attracted large numbers of disadvantaged students from all walks of life – even in pre-video recorder days when programmes transmitted at 6 am had to be watched at 6 am!

The creation of the 'binary' system

Between 1968 and 1973 a new approach to the expansion of higher education was implemented. 'Polytechnics' were created, mainly based on amalgamations of significantly sized technical colleges. Bristol, Teesside, Preston (later Lancashire) and Brighton Polytechnics were typical of these institutions. They were not new to higher education, having offered some degree-level and particularly higher diploma level teaching for many years. The new institutions were to be vocationally oriented and were to be predominantly teaching rather than research institutions. They remained under local authority control, usually under the local education authority which also controlled primary and secondary schools and colleges in its area.

As a result of this development, UK higher education developed as a 'binary' system. Quality assurance – for example, assurance of the quality of degrees – could not be left solely in the hands of sometimes small local education authorities and the polytechnics were not given the power to award their own degrees. Instead the Council for National Academic Awards (CNAA) was set up: the CNAA carried out regular visits to polytechnics to check on the standards of teaching, and students graduated with a CNAA award.

Although oriented towards teaching, the polytechnics gradually increased their postgraduate and research work, recognizing that involvement of staff and students in leading-edge developments in their field greatly enhanced the higher education experience. It has been argued that the vitality of the new sector – ironically that created *after* the 'new universities' of the 1960s – was the driving force behind most of the innovation in UK higher education in the succeeding quarter century: 'virtually all the innovations which have occurred in the internal life of higher education have been led by the Open University and the polytechnics' (Wagner, 1995).

Resource constraint and expansion: the creation of a single sector

By the end of the 1970s it was becoming clear that the justification for a binary system of higher education was wearing very thin. The polytechnics had established themselves as mature institutions with a national and international, rather than predominantly local and regional, role and the CNAA had ensured that the standards of their teaching and awards were on a par with those of the universities. They were establishing research reputations and many of the fields in which they excelled, such as business studies and art and design, were not only of increasing importance to the economy but were not well established in the traditional university sector. Their emphasis, during their formative years, on teaching had given them a much more student-centred ethos. Not least, their unit costs were lower – they were demonstrating, albeit sometimes with considerable pain because of their relatively poor resourcing, that mass higher education was both feasible and an economically viable proposition. Government control of their affairs had moved to the National Advisory Body (NAB), although it had a majority of local authority members. An issue of increasing concern, however, was that the name 'polytechnic', being peculiar to the UK, was not understood internationally and this put the polytechnics at a disadvantage compared with their university competitors.

The older universities did themselves no favours with government by their reaction to the funding crises of the early 1980s. The UGC had been forced to introduce a serious measure of accountability, and the Government had, as part of general reductions in public finance, reduced university budgets. In 1981, a cut of 15% was imposed. Instead of making the expected efficiency savings, some universities tried to maintain the 'unit of resource' (i.e. income per student) by cutting student numbers. Although this policy was soon abandoned, the damage had been done.

Later in the 1980s, external quality assurance was introduced into the university sector through subject reviews of teaching and through the first of a series of Research Assessment Exercises (RAE), carried out at approximately five-year intervals. Again, this introduced a further measure of accountability.

In 1987 a White Paper, *Meeting the Challenge*, was published leading to the 1988 Education Reform Act. The Act stated that higher education must

- serve the economy more effectively
- pursue basic scientific research and scholarship in the arts and humanities
- have closer links with industry and commerce, and promote enterprise.

The Act represented a significant step towards the creation of a single higher education sector. It resulted in the removal of the polytechnics from local authority control, with the establishment of the Polytechnics and Colleges Funding Council (PCFC). The UGC became the Universities Funding Council (UFC) at the same time. Once this change had been made, the logic of the binary divide was mortally wounded, and in 1992 the two sectors were merged with new funding councils for England, Scotland, Wales and Northern Ireland - the role of the last being undertaken by the Department of Education Northern Ireland (DENI). The Further and Higher Education Act of that year provided the legislation to enable the polytechnics to use the 'university' title if they so wished. All did so, although Anglia Polytechnic chose the curious amalgam of 'Anglia Polytechnic University'. The Act thus created a single higher education sector in the UK, with the former polytechnics and the former universities sharing essentially the same status and title. Expansion of student numbers was accelerated, and the colleges of further education were given autonomy from local authority control: the Further Education Funding Council (FEFC) was set up to channel government grants to them.

New directions: the Dearing Review

In 1996 the Government set up a major review of higher education. Under the chairmanship of Sir Ronald Dearing, the review examined the UK's higher education system in detail and made recommendations of changes that were needed to enable it to serve the national interest into the 21st century. First the committee set out its view of the purposes of higher education, building on the purposes set out by Robbins. It should:

- encourage and enable all students - whether they demonstrate the highest intellectual potential or whether they have struggled to reach the threshold of higher education - to achieve beyond their expectations
- safeguard the rigour of its awards, ensuring that the UK qualifications meet the needs of UK students and have standing throughout the world
- be at the leading edge of world practice in effective teaching and learning
- undertake research that matches the best in the world, and make its benefits available to the nation
- ensure that its support for regional and local communities is at least comparable to that provided by higher education in competitor nations
- sustain a culture which demands disciplined thinking, encourages curiosity, challenges existing ideas and generates new ones
- be part of the conscience of a democratic society, founded on respect for the rights of the individual and the responsibilities of the individual to society as a whole
- be explicit and clear in how it goes about its business, be accountable to students and to society and seek continuously to improve its own performance. (National Committee of Enquiry into Higher Education, 1997).

The Dearing recommendations included a continued increase in participation in higher education. At the time of the report this stood at 32% of school leavers and Dearing recommended that it should increase to 45%. Importantly the committee recommended that 'increasing' should include 'widening' of participation to groups in society then poorly represented in higher education, including ethnic minorities and people from lower socio-economic groups. A great deal of effort was expended in trying to find ways in which this expansion could be afforded, and in the end the committee recommended that fees should be introduced for all students, with means-tested support for those who were from low-income families.

Much of the expansion envisaged by Dearing would not take place in universities themselves but through franchise and other arrangements. Furthermore, the committee recommended that expansion should predominantly be of what it termed 'sub-degree' work, an unfortunate term for higher national diplomas and similar qualifications. The report also recommended actions to increase the use of information and communications technologies (ICTs) in teaching and learning, and the setting up of an Institute for Learning and Teaching, which would ensure that those teaching in universities were competent to do so. Dearing took evidence from employers of graduates and noted that many of them were critical of the workplace skills of new graduates. The committee therefore recommended that every graduate should be required to demonstrate competence in a number of 'key skills', including communication skills, numeracy, the use of IT and 'learning how to learn'.

The 2003 White Paper

In 2003 the UK government set out in a new White Paper what it termed a 'new vision' for higher education. Its main points were:

- Universities as creators of knowledge and 'engines' for applying new knowledge.
- Universities as educators, enabling students 'to live life to the full, through the acquisition of skills and through fostering imagination, creativity and contribution to society'.

- Although all universities should provide excellent teaching and should engage with under-represented groups, other aspects of mission would vary from institution to institution.
- The development of collaborations, both between universities and with other bodies.
- The support of those institutions which are world-class in research.
- Expansion to 50% participation by young people between the ages of 18–30.
- Development of new modes of study in response to student demand.
- Responsibility for funding shared between government (or, more accurately and as the White Paper put it, the taxpayer), students and 'others'.

This last point was particularly important, for it marked the culmination of a long debate about funding and whether universities should be allowed to set their own level of fees. The Vice-Chancellors broadly welcomed the proposals and they were enacted in the 2004 Higher Education Act. The result is that much higher fees are being introduced, although there are provisions for support for students from poorer families.

The Higher Education Academy

In 2004 a new organization came into being with the formation of the Higher Education Academy. It was created by the merger of the Institute for Learning and Teaching in Higher Education (ILTHE), the Learning and Teaching Support Network (LTSN), and the TQEF National Co-ordination Team (NCT). ILTHE had been created as a result of the Dearing recommendation that there should be a body with responsibility for promoting and enhancing teaching quality in higher education. Membership was, and remains under the ambit of the Academy, open to lecturers in higher education who can demonstrate their competence in teaching. The LTSN consists of a set of 24 subject centres and a generic centre, all providing resources and advice to higher education in matters relating to learning and teaching. As an example, the Centre for Information and Computer Sciences, which covers librarianship, is run from Loughborough and Ulster Universities. The NCT offers support for innovation in learning and teaching, particularly for a number of funded programmes, and supports institutions in the development of learning and teaching strategies.

University structures

Since universities are independent organizations, it is hardly surprising that their internal structures vary widely. The chief officer is normally known as the Vice-Chancellor (the Chancellorship being a largely honorary appointment often undertaken by a well-known public figure) although titles such as Principal are also found. Typically, major subject areas are headed by a Dean, who is responsible for a number of Departments or Schools grouped as a Faculty. At the Department/School level there are Heads, and it is here that teaching and research is organized in specific subject disciplines. The University will also have a number of administrative departments, ranging from the Registry through Human Resources and Finance to Estates, each headed by a senior member of staff. Libraries and computing services sit somewhere between the academic and the administrative departments since their role is directly related to learning and research but they do not have direct responsibility for students or programmes of study. Finally there will be a variety of centres, for example to promote eLearning or for specific research specialisms.

The funding and governance of higher education in the UK

Although the majority of funding for UK higher education comes from the government, the universities themselves are autonomous bodies operating under royal charters. As noted above, the requirement for accountability for the use of public funds has eroded the former independence that older universities enjoyed, and all institutions now face a variety of checks on the way in which funding is used and on the quality of their outputs, both teaching and research.

Although there are wide variations in the proportion of a university's income arising from each source, the following are the major sources of income of UK institutions:

• A block grant for teaching, based on student numbers, provided through one of the higher education funding councils.

- Student fees but with student contributions introduced for all undergraduate programmes in 1998, initially set at £1000 per annum but about to increase steeply as described above.
- Overseas student fees, typically set at a much higher level than those for home (which includes all EC countries) students.
- A block grant for research, again disbursed by the funding councils, based on the outcome of the Research Assessment Exercises held every five or so years in which each department is rated on a scale from 1 to 5*; the volume of research being undertaken, as well as its rating, counts in the calculation of the block grant.
- Funding attracted from the research councils (the Arts & Humanities Research Board, which will become a full Research Council in 2005, the Biotechnology & Biological Sciences Research Council, the Engineering & Physical Sciences Research Council, Economic & Social Research Council, the Medical Research Council, the Natural Environment Research Council and the Particle Physics & Astronomy Research Council). These funds are distributed on the basis of specific proposals for projects made by individual academic staff; the system of supporting research through both the research councils and the funding councils is known as the dual support system.
- Funding attracted from other bodies, usually for research but also for teaching and training. Such bodies include the European Commission, charitable foundations and private sector companies.

In addition to the budgets distributed by the funding councils, some funding is held back for central expenditure. The most significant service funded in this way is the Joint Information Systems Committee (JISC) which:

- Provides the Joint Academic Network (JANET), a high-speed wide-area network connecting all UK higher education institutions; various enhancements and developments over the years have been undertaken and these network features are known as SuperJANET. The current version, which will remain in place until the end of 2005, is SuperJANET4 and provides a core network backbone operating at 10 Gbit/s. JANET is an example of a National Research and Education

Network (NREN); other countries have similar provision, such as SURFNET5 in the Netherlands and CA*NET4 in Canada.

- Funds a wide variety of information-related services, including the national data centres and the Resource Discovery Network (RDN) – these are described in Chapter 5. These services are delivered within what is known as the JISC Information Environment.
- Funds a number of development activities, often by issuing a call for proposals for specific projects to institutions, which then choose whether or not to respond.
- Provides advice and leadership in a variety of ICT-related areas: for example, it is funding a UK office to undertake work on the US-led Instructional Management Systems (IMS) initiative, it has provided guidance on the development of information strategies by institutions and it issues advice on technical standards.
- Contributes to the development of a Common Information Environment (CIE), which aims to ensure that major public sectors use common standards and share development expertise.

Teaching and learning
Teaching and learning methods

The expansion of universities has been one of the driving forces behind changes in teaching and learning methods in higher education. Much has been written about 'student-centred learning' and there has certainly been a change in emphasis in the way in which students are taught, although it is notable that in most institutions there remains a very heavy emphasis on staff delivering lectures. Of course, what happens in those lectures may have changed – there is generally more interaction, with students encouraged to contribute and question – but nevertheless this time-honoured method of teaching remains dominant. At the same time, other methods have developed alongside – such as greater use of group work and, importantly for libraries, much greater emphasis on independent study. Because staff-student ratios have worsened, staff tend to be much less accessible to students than in the past and so students can be thrown more on their own devices. As a result, library staff can find that independent learning places greater strains on them as advisers and tutors – a role they are not always well prepared for or even well qualified to carry out.

For many years there has been discussion of the development of 'resource-based learning'. Although this term means different things to different people, at its heart lies the idea that much learning can take place through direct contact between learners and resources, such as documentary material. There has been considerable use of this approach in further education, especially through the development of open learning materials, but take-up of the idea in higher education has been much more limited. The eLib-funded IMPEL project (see Chapter 6) found that in only just over 10% of institutions was resource-based learning used in all faculties or departments, while over 40% reported that it was not used at all.

A further debate about learning which is still continuing concerns whether the aim should be to develop *competencies* or *knowledge*. Competence-based approaches are at the heart of the national vocational qualification (NVQ) system and are based on the idea that students should be able to demonstrate competence to undertake specific tasks, which taken together provide evidence of competence in a particular field. However, while at lower NVQ levels this is largely accepted, albeit with a few reservations, it is not clear that in higher education the demonstration of specific competencies is adequate, especially as the development of flexibility and, in Robbins' phrase, 'the powers of the mind' are paramount.

Modularization

Most UK universities now operate their undergraduate and taught postgraduate programmes as modular schemes, with students undertaking units or modules which may be an academic year, a term or a semester (there being two semesters per academic year, on the American model) in length. Usually there will be core modules which all students must take, and then a range of optional modules. The extent to which students' courses are prescribed varies – in some subjects there are very few options or 'electives', while in others students may 'pick and mix' from a wide range. The most flexible programmes do not lead to a named award (i.e. a degree or diploma in a named subject) but instead to a 'combined honours' or 'combined studies' award although these appear to be less popular than in the past. It is usual for degree courses to include a major project in the final year, and a similar, but more advanced, element will be found in nearly all postgraduate courses. Such projects, of course, place demands on the library for a broad range of resources – an issue we will consider in the next chapter.

Credit accumulation and transfer

There has long been concern that students' achievements in one institution should be transferable to another. Credit accumulation and transfer schemes (CATS) are designed to meet this need, allowing students to earn credits for each element of their course and accumulate these until they are eligible for an award, such as a diploma or degree. The credits should be designed to be transferable between institutions so that if students wish to complete their studies elsewhere they can take accumulated credits with them. To achieve this, universities must agree a common CATS currency.

Credit accumulation and transfer was in fact raised by the Robbins Committee in its recommendations, although little was done about it. The OU broke new ground by introducing credit-based units and in the 1980s the CNAA established its own credit transfer scheme. Yet the university system failed to adopt an agreed approach and in 1994 there was yet another attempt to do so, led by the Higher Education Quality Council (HEQC). The Dearing Report reiterated the need for a common system. Presently much attention is being paid to a pan-European model known as 'The Bologna Process'. This initiative takes its name from the Bologna Declaration signed by the education ministers of 29 countries in 1999 and is being followed up in a series of intergovernmental conferences. The UK has introduced a framework for higher education qualifications (Quality Assurance Agency for Higher Education, 2001a, 2001b) which is compliant with the Bologna principles.

Accreditation of prior learning

Although the majority of students entering UK higher education have qualified to do so through the 'A' level route, increasing numbers of mature entrants offer alternative evidence of their capabilities and potential. All universities are willing to consider such evidence, which usually comes under regulations concerning the accreditation of prior learning (APL) and accreditation of prior experiential learning (APEL), the latter recognizing that life experiences – such as work or raising a family – can provide an excellent grounding for academic study. It is important for staff of universities, including library staff, to recognize that this type of learning is different from, but not inferior to, traditional routes and may require different kinds of support.

Continuing professional development

Increasingly, students are returning to university to pursue their education beyond first degree level. Postgraduate courses may be split into two types – those which are 'end on' to a first degree and aim to raise the levels of knowledge and understanding of a subject above first degree level, and those which are 'conversion' courses, taking students who have graduated in one discipline and bringing them up to at least degree level, in another. Most postgraduate librarianship courses fall into the latter category, with the major dissertation required to reach Masters level then providing the further step up. Another category of provision is the short course, which may be for refreshing understanding or updating knowledge – such courses may form part of a formal programme of continuing professional development (CPD), which may also involve elements of experiential learning, action research and reflective practice. The differences between the various postgraduate and short courses are of course important when the university designs the support structures for students, including the library services.

Franchising

Since the late 1980s the practice of universities franchising their courses to other providers, usually further education colleges, has become widespread. The university, as the *franchiser*, retains the responsibility for quality assurance, for student numbers and for funding from the funding council. The college or other body, as the *franchisee*, is responsible for all elements of delivering the course, including such matters as library provision. Before permission is granted to the franchisee to recruit to the course, there will be a *validation event* at which its fitness to operate the course is examined in detail, and there will be *review* events at regular intervals. Some universities have franchised courses to institutions outside the UK, and there is no reason why this should not be successful, provided rigorous quality assurance procedures are in place and are used. A few cases where this has been neglected have given international franchising something of a bad name, but there are many excellent and successful examples of this practice.

Research
The practice of research

Research practice differs markedly between disciplines. In the sciences, technology and many of the social sciences the norm is for a team of researchers to work collaboratively, often involving colleagues from around the world. In the humanities the tradition of the individual scholar persists – this is not to say that such scholars work in isolation, for they exchange ideas and debate their findings at length; however, the focus tends to be more on the individual's contribution. Across most disciplines there has been a tendency in recent years for university researchers to work closely with those in industry, commerce and the professions and there is some evidence that the American practice whereby academics spend regular time in the private sector is developing in the UK.

The funding of research

Typically, UK universities derive the funding for their research from a mix of sources. The most important are:

- The block grant from the funding councils, in which the research funding is calculated by reference to the outcomes of the most recent Research Assessment Exercise.
- Funds from the Research Councils, obtained by competitive processes which involve researchers in making proposals, which are then *peer reviewed* (i.e. subject to scrutiny by experts in the field – the researchers' *peers*). Competition for such grants is fierce.
- Funds from other government agencies, including the European Commission's major research and development programmes – again this is usually through a competitive process involving peer review.
- Funds from a wide variety of private sector, charitable and private foundations and other bodies; for example, the Wellcome Foundation funds a large amount of medical research while the Rowntree and Nuffield Foundations fund work in the social sciences.

- Funding generated from consultancy and other services which exploit the expertise of the research team; a major issue for universities is their ability to transfer technological and other know-how to the private sector and to reap financial rewards for so doing. As we have seen above, the 2003 White Paper placed considerable emphasis on this role.

The quality of higher education

Quality has been a dominant theme in higher education in the UK for many years. Internal processes have been put in place so that institutions can be sure that their courses and research reach adequate standards (*quality assurance*), while external processes have been devised to check that they have adequate and effective internal processes (*quality audit*) and that there is an authoritative, national view on the quality of provision in each institution (*quality assessment*). (Note however that terminology is sometimes used rather loosely, and quality assurance may be used to mean quality assessment plus quality audit.) Anyone who doubts that there has been a remarkable improvement in the quality of UK research, teaching and learning is advised to re-read (or read) Kingsley Amis's *Lucky Jim* – satirical it may be, but it highlights just how much academic life has changed since the 1950s!

The system for assessing the quality of research, through the regular Research Assessment Exercises, is relatively well established, and involves each department in each university submitting its case at approximately five-yearly intervals. The case that is made includes a list of up to four key publications by each member of staff, an analysis of external research income attracted by the department, data on research student activity including the number of successful completions of research Masters degrees and doctorates, and a reflective analysis of the department's research culture and its strengths and weaknesses. In the last two Exercises departments have been graded on a scale which runs from 1 (meaning that there is no recognizable research of significance) to 5* (meaning a department of international excellence). Because an increasing number of departments are receiving the accolade of 5* status, the decision has been made to introduce a continuous grading scheme to replace the previous scale, thus enabling degrees of excellence to be identified. This will be implemented for the next RAE in 2008.

The quality assessment of learning and teaching has proved more problematic and has gone through a variety of changes over the years. The traditional approach has been through the *external examiner* system, whereby an academic from another institution scrutinizes practice – and in particular examination setting and marking – to ensure that equivalent standards were being applied across all universities. During the 1990s there was a system of subject assessment, operated by the funding councils, in which each department was assessed on six criteria – curriculum design and organization; teaching, learning and assessment; student progression and achievement; student support and guidance; learning resources; and quality management and enhancement – on a scale of 1 to 4. The cumulative result was thus a score out of 24. Any department receiving a 1 in any aspect would be deemed unsatisfactory and subject to another visit. On the other hand, overall 'excellence' would be rewarded with additional student numbers and therefore income.

Quality audit has been carried out on an institutional basis for some years, initially under the aegis of the Higher Education Quality Council, with new universities receiving *continuation audits* to bring audits of the early 1990s up to date. In 1997 a new Quality Assurance Agency for Higher Education (QAA) was set up to take over the responsibilities of the different agencies (HEQC had been owned by the universities rather than the funding councils, but the latter had been responsible for quality assurance in the institutions they funded), and consulted widely on a new teaching quality system which was to be based on subject benchmarks together with course outcome standards. Library support was included under the heading of 'learning resources'. Presently the system is based on institutional audits which are undertaken on a six-year cycle. Further information is available on the QAA website at www.qaa.ac.uk/aboutqaa/qaaintro/ intro.htm.

Further education and the Kennedy Report

Further education (FE) has always been difficult to define, since FE colleges cover a remarkable spectrum of work from special needs teaching for people with learning difficulties to postgraduate training and even research. The Kennedy Committee (see below) memorably defined further education as 'everything that does not happen in schools or universities'.

After being released from local authority control in 1992, further education colleges found themselves operating in a market in which competition between educational providers was encouraged. Just as in higher education, growth was massive but was accompanied by major economies and increases in efficiency. One of the problems with this market-driven approach was that instead of producing a national system of further education geared to national needs, it provoked colleges into competing to attract students and into offering only courses which would both attract students and be 'profitable'. As a result, some groups were being excluded from full participation.

In December 1994, the Further Education Funding Council set up a committee, chaired by Helena Kennedy QC, to advise it – and through it, government – on widening participation in further education. Its final report, *Learning Works*, was published in June 1997 (Further Education Funding Council, 1997). Unlike the multi-volume Dearing Report, *Learning Works* is a short document, distilling its argument and conclusions into little more than 100 A5 pages. It is arguable, however, that it was more influential than Dearing.

The Kennedy Report made a strong case that the needs of the country would best be served by widening participation in education, with further education at the heart of that strategy. It explicitly stated that funding should be switched from higher to further education to enable this to happen, although this suggestion was not to be accepted by government. Most importantly, Kennedy placed further education at the heart of the movement to achieve lifelong learning for all: when the Labour Government took office in May 1997, with its mantra of 'education, education, education', the Kennedy Report was almost immediately on ministers' desks.

Lifelong learning

A major concern for the UK government, and for governments around the world, is how to build a society where all citizens can develop their full potential and which has at its disposal the skills and knowledge to thrive in the increasingly competitive world economy. One of the main policy planks which has been put in place to achieve these goals is the encouragement of lifelong learning for all. 1996 was the European Year of Lifelong Learning and a study undertaken during that year revealed that only a third of adults in England and Wales had undertaken any form of learning during the previous three years (Tuckett, 1997). In a fast-changing world, where skills learned only months ago can be outdated, this was not a reassuring picture.

In recent years a series of initiatives has been launched to address this situation. The Government's response to the Dearing and Kennedy Reports was incorporated in this wider agenda, the overall policy being published in a Green Paper, *The Learning Age* (DfEE, 1998a), which set out seven principles for action:

- extending learning opportunities
- making education and training more flexible and more accessible
- removing barriers to learning
- investing in young people, to motivate and enable as many as possible to study beyond the age of 16
- improving the quality, responsiveness and local accountability of FE
- securing improvements in information on learning
- rebalancing the partnership for investment in learning, by encouraging greater employer contributions.

To accompany the Green Paper the Government published its formal responses to the Dearing and Kennedy Reports (DfEE, 1998b; DfEE, 1998c). For higher education the key issues would be:

- increasing and widening participation
- offering opportunities for mature students
- increasing HE's contribution to the economy
- greater collaboration both with other institutions and with 'the world of work'
- exploiting new technology and flexible delivery in order to become more accessible and to use facilities more efficiently, e.g. through longer opening hours.

An early action of government was to set up the National Advisory Group for Continuing Education and Lifelong Learning. Chaired by Professor R. H. Fryer, the group issued its first report in November 1997, *Learning for the Twenty-First Century* (National Advisory Group for Continuing Education and Lifelong Learning, 1997). The main thrust of this report lies in the need to develop a culture of lifelong learning for all:

> Above all, a vision of a learning culture will envisage learning as a normal, accessible, productive and enjoyable (if demanding) feature of everyday life for all people, throughout their lives. It will provide stimulus and opportunities for people to be able to make use of information, skills and knowledge to improve their own lives and those of their loved ones, fellow citizens and people in other countries. Lifelong learning can change people's lives, even transform them.

A flurry of actions accompanied these reports: the establishment of the *National Grid for Learning* and the *University for Industry* (later marketed as learndirect when it was realized that it was not a university and not limited to 'industry'!) and the release of significant amounts of funding from the National Lottery, for example for the training of teachers and librarians in ICT skills.

Creating Learning Cultures: next steps in achieving the learning age was the second report of the National Advisory Group for Continuing Education and Lifelong Learning, published in 1999 (National Advisory Group for Continuing Education and Lifelong Learning, 1999). It reviewed progress since the publication of *The Learning Age* and made new recommendations, including that 'government should instigate a major, multifaceted campaign to promote lifelong learning and the development of learning cultures' and that further work should be undertaken on 'the role and contribution of libraries and museums in lifelong learning'.

A further 1999 publication, *Learning to Succeed*, set out the Government's overall vision:

> To build a culture of learning which will underpin national competitiveness and personal prosperity, encourage creativity and innovation and help build a cohesive society. (DfEE, 1999)

As we have seen, four years later, in early 2003, the Government published its new White Paper on higher education (Department for Education and Skills, 2003). Whether it has yet achieved the 1999 vision for lifelong learning is a matter for debate.

Conclusion

Higher education grew enormously during the 20th century, the number of institutions and the number of students increasing through a series of planned expansions until by the century's end the United Kingdom had a truly national, mass higher education system. However, most of these changes occurred towards the century's end and it is already clear that the pace of change will be no less frenetic in the 21st century. New methods of delivering education, most notably through the application of information and communications technologies, have so far given only a hint of what is to come. However, it seems unlikely that education will become the preserve of technology, for at heart it is a social process, and the challenge for institutions and individuals will be to create an effective blend of technology and social interaction in order that higher education may take its place in the wider range of lifelong learning opportunities.

Thus the challenges facing 21st century universities and colleges are profound, but they confront them from a strong base and with government commitment to their basic mission. However, they need to widen participation, to achieve a higher level technology and knowledge transfer to the wider economy, to maintain and where possible enhance standards and to compete on a world stage. Their libraries can support the achievement of excellence in all these fields.

References

Committee on Higher Education (1963) *Higher Education: report of the Committee appointed by the Prime Minister under the chairmanship of Lord Robbins 1961-1963* (Robbins Report), Cmnd 2154, HMSO.

Department for Education and Employment (1998a) *The Learning Age*, Department for Education and Employment.

Department for Education and Employment (1998b) *The Learning Age: higher education for the 21st century: response to the Dearing Report*, Department for Education and Employment.

Department for Education and Employment (1998c) *The Learning Age: further education for the 21st century: response to the Dearing Report*, Department for Education and Employment.

Department for Education and Employment (1999) *Learning to Succeed: a new framework for post-16 learning*, Department for Education and Employment.

Department for Education and Skills (2003) *The Future of Higher Education*, www.dfes.gov.uk/hegateway/hereform/index.cfm?cid=2.

Further Education Funding Council (1997) *Learning Works: widening participation in further education* (Kennedy Report), Further Education Funding Council.

National Advisory Group for Continuing Education and Lifelong Learning (1997) *Learning for the Twenty-first Century: first report of the National Advisory Group for Continuing Education and Lifelong Learning* (Fryer Report), Report PP62/31634/1297/33, Department for Education and Employment.

National Advisory Group for Continuing Education and Lifelong Learning (1999) *Creating Learning Cultures: next steps in achieving the learning age*, Department for Education and Employment.

National Committee of Inquiry into Higher Education (1997) *Higher Education in the Learning Society* (The Dearing Report), HMSO.

Perkin, H. (1984) The Historical Perspective. In B. R. Clark (ed.), *Perspectives on Higher Education: eight disciplinary and comparative views*, University of California Press, 17-55.

Quality Assurance Agency for Higher Education (2001a) *The Framework for Higher Education Qualifications in England, Wales and Northern Ireland*, www.qaa.ac.uk/crntwork/nqf/ewni2001/contents.htm.

Quality Assurance Agency for Higher Education (2001b) *The Framework for Qualifications of Higher Education Institutions in Scotland*, www.qaa.ac.uk/crntwork/nqf/scotfw2001/contents.htm.

Tuckett, A. (1997) *Lifelong Learning in England and Wales: an overview and guide to issues arising from the European Year of Lifelong Learning*, NIACE.

Wagner, L. (1995) A Thirty-year Perspective: from the sixties to the nineties, In Schuller, T. (ed.), *The Changing University*, SRHE/Open University Press, 15-24.

Further reading

The *Times Higher Education Supplement* (weekly) is essential reading for anyone interested in higher education in the UK. See www.thes.co.uk/.

2

The history of higher education libraries

Introduction

Chapter 1 examined the history of academic institutions. In this chapter the focus will turn to libraries, again looking at origins and development. The aim is to characterize the library services which are in existence in academic institutions today. In so doing, we will examine the key government and other reports and initiatives which have influenced and shaped the academic library sector as a whole, concentrating especially on those which occurred in the final decade of the 20th century and the first decade of the 21st (so far!), and thus setting the scene for the academic libraries of today.

Academic libraries in pre-modern times

Libraries existed in the ancient world, the most celebrated being those at Nineveh, created in the seventh century BC, and - most famous of all - the library at Alexandria in Egypt created by Ptolemy Soter some time around 300 BC. The latter contained an unparalleled collection of papyrus rolls consisting of the majority of mankind's recorded knowledge. The loss of the Great Library of Alexandria - probably destroyed in the late 4th century CE - resulted quite literally in the loss of much human knowledge and it is a matter of speculation as to how world history might have unfolded had its treasures remained available - a lesson in the importance of preservation which should not be ignored today.

The history of modern libraries may be traced to that founded by Aristotle - pre-dating the Alexandrian library - which was eventually moved to Rome. Ollé (1967) suggests that the first public library opened in Rome in c. 37 BC, describing such foundations as 'reference libraries attached to temples'. Such libraries, some of which were of significant size, continued until the fall of the Roman Empire in the West and survived much later in the East. So, for example, ancient Islamic collections survived, some as late as the Ottoman Empire, although much was lost to war and natural disaster.

There were no great libraries in Europe in the early Middle Ages to rival those of Nineveh and Alexandria of the first millennium BC. What survived throughout the period from the destruction of the Roman Empire through to the 13th century were small - tiny by today's standards - collections of manuscripts in monasteries scattered across the continent, together with collections in private hands. It would be quite rare for the library to occupy a separate room, never mind its own building. Copies of manuscripts were made laboriously by hand and were treasured and closely guarded. As Thompson (1977) points out, 'the common word for library in the early Middle Ages was *armarium*, the name for the bookchest where the books were kept; and the librarian of such a collection was known as the *armarius*'.

The college or university libraries were equally small, and grew very slowly. Cambridge University Library had only 122 volumes in 1424, but the number was starting to grow - by copying, by purchase, but most importantly by donations and gifts. Because each copy was literally unique, and there were inevitably variations between copies of the same work, the standing of a monastery or cathedral could be measured by the volumes which its library held. Scholars would travel from library to library to consult rare and valuable manuscripts - the opposite of today's interlibrary loan systems, under which the books travel to the users!

The revolution which enabled the medieval libraries to expand was, of course, the invention of printing using movable type by Johannes Gutenberg in Germany in the mid-15th century. Printing, although setting up was itself a laborious process, allowed multiple copies to be produced and then sold and thus dispersed around the libraries of Europe. Each copy was to all intents and purposes identical, so that a collection in one place could be mirrored by one elsewhere. Within 50 years the commercial production of manuscripts had all but ceased.

Books remained costly and comparatively rare for some time, however. Incunabula (i.e. books printed before 1500) were produced in small numbers - usually a few hundred copies - and fetched high prices in contemporary terms. However, in the 16th century production increased. Estimates vary, but Johnson (1970) suggests that about 100,000 titles were produced in the 16th century. At the same time, the number of copies of each title being produced was increasing. During the 17th and 18th centuries print runs of 2000–3000 copies would be typical, while in the 19th century the number grew rapidly and a run of a million copies was, if not commonplace, not unusual.

The impact of these changes on the libraries of universities during the late medieval period was profound. The Bodleian Library at Oxford University, to take one example, saw its collections increase in size to approximately 16,000 volumes by 1620, and to 30,000 by 1700. The nature of these libraries started to change with the advent of the printed book. The classics and theological works remained significant, but they were joined by a wide diversity of other subjects and for the first time journals became important. With the development of learned societies, the communication of observations, research results, etc. became more formalized and in January 1665 *Le Journal des Savants* was published in France, followed three months later by the *Philosophical Transactions* of the Royal Society in England. Both were published regularly (albeit with interruptions) and contained several scholarly papers in each issue together with other material: the first issue of the *Philosophical Transactions* contained a bibliography of important monographs, for example.

The 18th century saw significant developments, not least the foundation of the British Museum Library in 1759. The ready availability of printed books led also to the establishment of subscription libraries and book clubs, some of which – like the journals – were based on learned societies. However, the university libraries played a relatively minor part in this expansion of recorded knowledge.

The 19th century

Just as the number of institutions which we would today call universities grew throughout the 19th century, so too did the number and size of their libraries. If we turn away from the 'ancient' universities and look to other types of institution, it is interesting to note the importance of libraries. As we have seen in Chapter 1, the mechanics' institutes typically established a library as part of their core service. Although these libraries, and their reading rooms, were small and highly selective in the books they stocked, they pointed to a belief in libraries as a major agent of education. That their demise in this role – becoming rather poorly resourced departments of technical colleges – should be caused by the public library movement is somewhat ironic.

While the libraries of the ancient universities developed slowly throughout the century, those of the newer foundations were generally small, underfunded and poorly staffed. At this time librarianship was not regarded as a separate profession in universities, and a senior academic would normally discharge the role of 'librarian' – a situation which still pertains in some Oxbridge colleges. While a few remarkable individuals – like Edward Nicholson at the Bodleian, who is also generally acknowledged as the founder of The Library Association – were able to make a significant impact, in his case by undertaking a thorough reorganization of his library, these were very much the exception.

The early 20th century

Libraries continued to grow gradually during the early years of the 20th century, but it became apparent that provision varied enormously between institutions. The UGC investigated the situation and in a report published in 1921 made one of the most supportive and appreciative statements about libraries ever to emerge from a quasi-government body:

> The character and efficiency of a university may be gauged by its treatment of its central organ – the library. We regard the fullest provision for library maintenance as the primary and most vital need in the equipment of a university.   (University Grants Committee, 1921)

However, in part because of the degree of autonomy enjoyed by the universities and in part because of the severe economic recession of the 1920s and 1930s followed by World War 2, little was done to ensure that a minimum standard of library provision was made, and as late as the 1950s and even early 1960s provision could be minimal. It was not until the new universities were being founded that a systematic review of provision was undertaken in a thorough investigation by a committee chaired by Dr Thomas Parry.

The Parry Report

The Committee on Libraries of the UGC, which reported in 1967 and whose final report is known as the Parry Report after its chairman, was undoubtedly influenced by the new thinking about academic libraries which had been brought about by the creation of new universities (University Grants Committee, 1967). For the first time, librarians had been given a clean sheet of paper on which to plan a library from scratch. The library had been regarded by the vice-chancellors and senior staff of these new institutions as symbolic of the universities themselves, and without exception the library was placed centrally on the campus, and designed to reflect the dynamic ethos of the new universities.

The Parry Committee's investigations were wide-ranging, and entirely supportive of excellence in academic library provision. It recognized that libraries are expensive to build and maintain, and recommended that universities should devote a minimum of around 6% of their revenue expenditure to the library:

> The annual cost . . . of library provision in a university of medium size would amount to about six per cent of the budget of such a university. Circumstances vary, and it would be undesirable and impractical to impose standards centrally, but we believe that this represents a standard below which British university libraries should not be allowed to fall.

Not surprisingly, this figure was much quoted by librarians in their budget negotiations, although few reached this level consistently.

A further issue which exercised the committee was that of library co-operation. It attempted to steer a course between each library's need to be self-sufficient in its holdings – then almost an article of faith – and the obvious benefits of sharing those resources which were little in demand. Interestingly, the Parry Report suggested that the British Museum should be seen as the 'apex' of the academic library system in the UK.

Expansion and consolidation: from Parry to Atkinson

If the 1960s saw the building of new libraries and the rapid expansion of collections, the 1970s and 1980s were decades of consolidation and increasing resource constraint. The new universities of the 1960s were given generous capital grants to enable them to create library collections; in the 1970s the same was not true of the polytechnics, although great efforts were made to expand collections and to build suitable library accommodation for the rapidly expanding numbers of higher education students. However, as the economic climate in the country worsened following the 1973-4 oil crisis so pressure on budgets became ever tighter, and across both sectors libraries felt the effects. As a result, there was very considerable disparity in the range and depth of services offered by higher education libraries: it was perhaps not surprising that, in general, the older the institution, the better the collection.

In 1975 the UGC set up a working party on capital provision for university libraries to report on how the committee should deal with the situation in which it had become clear that it would be impossible to fund all the requests for additional library space, even in the university sector – the report did not, of course, address the situation in the polytechnics. The Atkinson Report, as it became known, reiterated that 'the library is the core of a university', but went on to propose what at the time appeared a highly controversial concept, of 'a "self-renewing" library in which new accessions would be relieved by the withdrawal of obsolete or unconsulted material to other stores' (University Grants Committee, 1976). The report recommended new space norms for libraries, including norms for the provision of reserve stores, and urged greater co-operation and reliance on interlibrary loan. Typical of the reactions from librarians was this comment from Norman Higham, then University Librarian at Bristol:

> If the library is full, and the space limit of those who set the rules (the UGC in Britain) . . . has been reached, it is one book out for every book in, new books for old . . . Not only the reserve store, but the library itself would be a transit camp between acquisition and obsolescence. Consumer durables may have a predictable obsolescence but books do not, and we should find ourselves discarding books which we wanted to keep.   (Higham, 1980)

However, university librarians did not come up with any real alternative, and the pleas for ever-expanding libraries on every university campus were never realistic. In the event, libraries struggled on, some new buildings were erected and many found ways of expanding offsite storage. Since, throughout the 1980s, bookfunds were cut back the anticipated expansion was not as rapid as some had feared and it was only after the university and polytechnic sectors had merged that the issue of library space again came to the fore – but this time in a very different guise.

The Follett Report
Background

In 1992 the four higher education funding councils set up a major review of university library provision under the chairmanship of Sir Brian Follett, the then Vice-Chancellor of the University of Warwick. The committee itself was composed of both eminent librarians and university leaders, together with the President of the British Academy, Sir Anthony Kenny; the Librarian of the National Library of Wales, Brynley Roberts; the Director General of the British Library's Document Supply Service, David Russon; the Chief Executive of the Oxford University Press, Sir Roger Elliott; and the Director of Policy of the Higher Education Funding Council for England, Bahram Bekhradnia.

The terms of reference of the Follett Committee, as it became known, were:

> Taking into account
> a)   the planned expansion of higher education
> b)   the current and potential impact of IT on information provision
> c)   the possibilities of greater co-operation and sharing of capital and recurrent resources
> >   (i)   to investigate the future national needs for the development of library and information resources including operational and study space requirements for teaching and research in HE institutions, and
> >   (ii)   to identify ways to meet those needs.

The Committee reported in December 1993 and made a series of extremely significant recommendations, which were rapidly accepted by the funding councils (Higher Education Funding Council for England, Scottish Higher Education Funding Council, Higher Education Funding Council for Wales and the Department of Education for Northern Ireland, 1993). Additional funding was found to enable two areas in particular to be addressed as national priorities: the development of library buildings, whether through refurbishment and expansion, or through new building; and a programme of development to enable the exploitation of the potential of information technology. This second area resulted in the establishment of the Electronic Libraries Programme (eLib), described in Chapter 5.

Evidence

The Follett Committee assembled an impressive range of evidence to support its recommendations. The massive expansion of student numbers was one of the starting points: between 1988-9 and 1992-3 the number of full-time equivalent undergraduate students in British universities had grown from 517,000 to 811,000, a rise of 57%. The committee noted that, while this growth in participation had been welcomed on all sides, it had occurred at a time when institutions were being expected to work with reduced annual revenue budgets (so-called 'efficiency gains') and in a situation where there was very little funding available for capital building projects. For libraries, this had resulted in a situation where space for both readers and stock, the number of books and periodicals available, and the ability of staff to cope with increased and more diverse demand were all under pressure. As if this was not enough, libraries were facing increases in their costs far above the annual rate of general inflation. For example, between 1980-1 and 1991-2, the retail price index (RPI) had risen by 71%, library spending on periodicals had risen by 111% but the actual prices of periodicals had risen by almost 300% - cancellation of titles had been widespread. While some of these differences could legitimately be put down to increased efficiency (for example, libraries ceasing to subscribe to periodicals which were very little used), they indicated a clear problem which could not be allowed to continue unchecked.

The committee also drew attention to the impact on libraries of changes in teaching and learning methods in institutions. For example:

- increasing proportions of mature and part-time students, who tended to make different demands on libraries - for example a mature student with family responsibilities might need different loan arrangements from the norm
- modularization of degree courses, which altered the ways in which stock was used

- a change in perspective towards the student as a user and the library as a service provider, with concomitant changes in expectations
- changing learning methods which 'put more stress on student centred learning, and require the coherent development of learning and information resources of which libraries are a part'
- a decline in book purchasing by students, partly due to changes in the student support system, which led to greater demand on library stock, especially for heavily used *core* texts.

Although researchers' library needs had not featured prominently in the terms of reference or underlying justification for the committee's establishment, considerable attention was paid to those issues too. Clearly the reduction in libraries' real purchasing power was having an impact on researchers, although statistical evidence showed that libraries had generally increased the proportion of their funding being spent on periodicals at the expense of books – not that it should be assumed that researchers only use periodicals and students only use books. Again, however, changes in higher education in general were having an impact: the funding councils had introduced the Research Assessment Exercises (RAE) which were resulting in greater selectivity of funding. Departments were assessed to determine the quality of their research, and those receiving the highest gradings received a greater share of available resources. As a result, institutions found the concentration of their research shifting between subjects, and library support needed to be equally flexible. In some areas, where a 'well-found' library (i.e. one with in-depth collections) was crucial to research in the discipline, the need to protect RAE ratings was putting impossible demands on underfunded libraries.

The final area on which the Committee concentrated was that of the potential of information technology (IT), noting:

> The business of libraries is the provision and management of information, and developments in technology which facilitate these operations have opened up many new possibilities, as well as creating many new demands on libraries. Some of these developments have potentially very wide-ranging implications. They may, for instance, facilitate resource sharing and exchange, help to involve libraries and their staff directly in new forms of technologically based

teaching and learning, and encourage a change in the role of the library to become a means of access to information wherever it is held.

Two other issues concerned the committee. First it noted that the higher education sector in the UK had become very heterogeneous. In other words, there was enormous diversity between institutions: some were small, specialist colleges, some were among the largest universities in Europe; some were ancient foundations, others were modern creations with entirely different cultures. The committee, in recognizing this diversity, wisely stated that 'no single blueprint and no simple prescription can be developed to fit the many different types of libraries in higher education'. The second issue was that of copyright, which was seen as unduly restricting the use of material, much of it produced by the universities themselves.

Recommendations

In all, the committee made 46 recommendations of varying significance. They fell under the following headings:

1 *Information strategies.* It was recommended that every institution should develop an 'information strategy' which would set out its approach to the provision and management of information throughout the institution. It is important to note that these strategies were not 'information technology strategies' (though it would prove an uphill struggle to persuade some institutions that this was the case) and they were not 'library strategies', though they would include both of these. They would examine the acquisition, creation, management and use of information, whether for teaching, research or administrative purposes, throughout the institution, including its information relationships with external agencies, and set out a clear development strategy. Information strategies are discussed in the context of the academic library in Chapter 3.

2 *Library expenditure.* A suggestion that libraries should be directly funded by the funding councils, rather than through their parent institutions, was rejected. The committee instead recommended that each institution should review the level of spending on its library and the balance between different elements of that expenditure.

Interestingly, and arising out of discussions on the services being made available to students, there was a specific recommendation that institutions should review their expenditure on short loan collections.

3 *Performance indicators.* The committee recommended that further work be done on developing a set of performance indicators for libraries, and that these should be used in internal management. The development of performance indicators for academic libraries is discussed further in Chapter 12.

4 *Staffing and staff management.* A separate report, commissioned by the committee, had looked at staff management and staff development issues – the Fielden Report (John Fielden Consultancy, 1993). These issues are discussed in Chapter 6.

5 *Purchasing.* The committee's recommendations were rather weak in this area. They recommended investigation of the scope for further application of co-operative purchasing, and suggested that joint action with the Association of American Universities should be attempted to influence the periodicals market.

6 *Quality assessment and quality audit.* Mindful of the growing demand for accountability for the use of public funds and the increasing use of quality assurance processes, the committee recommended that library quality should be explicitly addressed when the Higher Education Quality Council (HEQC) and the funding councils audited and assessed teaching quality. A particular issue should be the effectiveness of liaison between the library staff and the teaching staff.

7 *Space and space management.* One of the committee's major recommendations was that a total of £140 million should be spent on library buildings, with £50 million being provided by the funding councils and the remainder by institutions. A number of other recommendations in this area included greater use of high density storage and reviews by institutions of their libraries' opening hours.

8 *Library co-operation in support of teaching.* Here it was recommended that £0.5 million should be provided for the development of co-operative arrangements between libraries to support teaching.

9 *Library provision and the needs of researchers.* In addition to calling for the development of a national strategy on research support, the committee recommended that, in exchange for continuation and expansion of the then current arrangements for special funding for

legal deposit and other major libraries, such as those of Oxford and Cambridge Universities, free access to such collections should be available to all UK university researchers. Up to £10 million a year should be provided by the funding councils to support research libraries with significant specialized collections in the humanities to enable them to offer such access.

10 *Information technology*. The IT-related recommendations of the committee were probably the most significant in the long term. They recommended that funding, totalling £14 million, should be invested by the funding councils in a programme of development which would include:

- network navigation tools, including subject-based approaches
- the development of standards
- electronic document delivery projects
- digitization of out-of-copyright books and journals
- electronic journal demonstrator projects
- the creation of customizable electronic texts
- assessment of the feasibility of establishing an 'Arts and Humanities Datacentre'
- the development of the Consortium of University Research Libraries (CURL) database and its conversion to a national online public access catalogue (OPAC)
- a study of the requirement for a national retrospective catalogue conversion programme
- demonstrations of the potential of integrated bibliographic databases, for example for course material
- a programme of awareness raising and training for librarians
- the exploration of the development of a management information system specification which would enable libraries to be integrated into institutional systems.

A remarkable feature of the Follett Committee's recommendations is that by far the majority of them were to be implemented over the following years. The story of the changes brought about through the committee's work will recur in later chapters, but it should be noted here that it introduced a new prominence for libraries in institutional and funding council thinking. Librarians dominated the key advisory sub-committees of the Joint Information Systems Committee (JISC), the body charged with delivering networked information and other services to higher education, and later to further education as well. Follett also provided the platform from which librarians were able to play a leading role in many of the most far-reaching IT-based developments in UK universities and created a situation in which, in a period of austerity, virtually the only new buildings erected on UK campuses were libraries. Its significance can therefore hardly be overestimated.

Academic libraries in the 1990s

Although the Follett Report and its aftermath dominated the development of academic libraries in the 1990s, especially through the Electronic Libraries Programme (eLib), a number of other significant factors were at work. Institutions were continuing to expand their student numbers and to compete for recognition of research excellence. ICTs were starting to play a larger part in institutional thinking, and the IT capability - in terms of applications and of hardware and bandwidth - both of individual institutions and of the sector as a whole was increasing. International collaboration was becoming more significant, especially for research teams, raising questions about library support.

Of particular significance has been a major initiative amongst academic librarians to foster what has been called 'academic integration', defined by Heery and Morgan (1996) as 'the nurturing of an active partnership between the library, academic departments and other institutional services in a wide range of liaison activities which respond to the information needs of the academic community'. The enthusiasm of libraries for such partnerships has not always, however, been reflected by that of academic staff.

The issue of lifelong learning also started to have an impact on academic libraries. An eLib supporting study looked at how libraries might need to change their services and the ways they were being delivered in order to provide the necessary support to lifelong learners. Among its recommendations were:

1   There should be continued encouragement at the highest level for co-operative approaches to comprehensive library provision suitable for supporting lifelong learners.
2   There is a need for more experimental work on the development of new, networked learning environments which would include the 'library' elements of support.
3   All academic library managers need an in-depth understanding of both the theory and practice of learning and the leading edge of network applications, especially those related to information systems.
4   The contribution which libraries make to lifelong learning has been insufficiently studied. Work should be undertaken to assess the value of libraries to lifelong learners and the impact which their services have on lifelong learning in general.
5   Institutions and their libraries should review their existing services, including their participation in co-operative arrangements, to determine whether they meet the needs of non-traditional lifelong learners.
6   The teaching of information skills should be reviewed to ensure that lifelong learners, and especially those whose exposure to the institution will be in short bursts, will be adequately equipped to undertake their courses and exploit information resources.
7   Librarians should consider whether a well-designed professional development programme designed to inform professional library staff about learning theory and research on effective learning could be launched.
8   Librarians should consider and debate with suppliers new licensing arrangements for access to electronic resources which, while protecting suppliers' legitimate interests, do not disadvantage off-campus learners.
    (Brophy, Craven and Fisher, 1998)

The Anderson Report

In 1994, following mounting concern about the maintenance of and access to research collections and responding to a specific recommendation of the Follett Report, a further committee was set up under the chairmanship of Professor Michael Anderson of Edinburgh University. The report of this body (Joint Funding Councils' Library Review, 1996) stressed the need for all major libraries in the UK to co-operate to ensure that researchers had adequate support and made a number of specific recommendations including:

- that universities should address the issue of library support for research in their information strategies, in their submissions under the Research Assessment Exercises and in bids for research funding made to the research councils
- that universities should consider making funds available to allow their researchers to travel to significant collections as an alternative to their own collection building
- that a national retentions policy should be created to ensure that at least one copy of older research materials was retained
- that collaborative arrangements between universities should be encouraged
- that there was a need to explore whether a system of recompensing those universities which faced significant additional costs in providing library services to researchers from other institutions should be introduced.

One of the outcomes of the Anderson Report was the establishment of the *Research Support Libraries Programme (RSLP)*. This major programme, funded at £30 million over three years (academic years 1999-2002), had four strands:

- supporting access to major holdings libraries
- collaborative collection management projects
- research support for humanities and social science collections
- targeted retrospective conversion of catalogues.

Examples of projects funded by RSLP include Glasgow University's GASHE (Gateway to Archives of Scottish Higher Education), Manchester Metropolitan University's Design Council Slide Collection Cataloguing and Digitization project, an Edinburgh University project entitled 'Finding the right clinical notes: improving access to personal health records in Scotland 1600-1994' and Nottingham University's EGIL (Electronic Gateway for Icelandic Literature). In addition a conservation unit at Dundee University was funded and the UK Office for Library and Information Networking (UKOLN) undertook work on collection descriptions.

The Research Libraries Network (RLN)

The Research Support Libraries Group (RSLG – not to be confused with the RSLP) was set up in 2001 to 'make recommendations to the HE Funding Bodies, the British Library and the national libraries of Scotland and Wales on a national strategic framework and mechanisms for promoting collaboration in, and integration of the development and provision of library collections, their long-term management, and services to support research' (RSLG, 2001). Again chaired by Sir Brian Follett, the Group sought ways to underpin the library contribution to the scholarly communication process which is at the heart of academic research.

The Report of the Group, published in March 2003, provided an incisive analysis of the provision of library resources to researchers in the UK and crucially recognized that a considerable proportion of those researchers were based outside academic institutions, for example in industry. It came to the conclusion that solutions to the problems it identified, which included the rapid but uneven development of electronic publication and electronic delivery, would have to be cross-sectoral. In the view of the Group, the biggest problem, once this situation was identified, was the lack of strategic direction on a national scale. Its key recommendation, therefore, was that a new body should be created, to be called the Research Libraries Network (RLN), which would carry out a strategic planning and co-ordination role. Alongside the universities themselves, the British Library and the national libraries of Scotland and Wales would be key players.

The funding councils and the research councils deliberated for a considerable time over the report, but in summer 2004 it was announced that the RLN would go ahead, with initial funding of £3 million. The executive of the RLN is based at the British Library. The announcement suggested that:

> Early emphasis is likely to be on improved knowledge of and access to existing resources (for example, by developing search tools and 'union catalogues' which give a single point of access to a number of different collections). Future potential workstreams include collaborative work on developing and preserving digital archives, maximising access for professional researchers to key collections, and working towards collaborative development of collections to ensure access to the widest possible range of research materials.   (HEFCE, 2004)

Conclusion

There is no doubt that academic libraries are changing rapidly, finding new roles and new ways to play traditional roles. It is remarkable that those charged with the planning and strategic management of higher education in the UK have spent so much time and energy on the affairs of libraries and on securing their future. For librarians the challenge remains of delivering services in a rapidly changing, high technology world where information is no longer in short supply, but services must compete for the attention of their potential users. Collaboration has now been signalled as the way forward.

References

Brophy, P., Craven, J. and Fisher, S. (1998) *The Development of UK Academic Library Services in the Context of Lifelong Learning*, Library Information Technology Centre on behalf of JISC.

Heery, M. and Morgan, S. (1996) *Practical Strategies for the Modern Academic Library*, Aslib.

Higham, N. (1980) *The Library in the University: observations on a service*, André Deutsch.

Higher Education Funding Council for England (2004) *£3 Million National Framework for UK Research Information Announced*, Bristol, HEFCE, www.hefce.ac.uk/news/hefce/2004/rln.asp.

Higher Education Funding Council for England, Scottish Higher Education Funding Council, Higher Education Funding Council for Wales and the Department of Education for Northern Ireland (1993) *Joint Funding Councils' Libraries Review Group: report* (Follett Report), HEFCE.

Independent (1999) Longest Conflict in British History Ends at the Eleventh Hour of the Century, *Independent* (3 December 1999), 2.

John Fielden Consultancy (1993) *Supporting Expansion. A report on human resource management in academic libraries, for the Joint Funding Councils' Libraries Review Group* (Fielden Report), HEFCE.

Johnson, E. D. (1970) *History of Libraries in the Western World*, 2nd edn, Scarecrow.

Joint Funding Councils' Library Review Group (1996) *Report of the Group on a National/regional Strategy for Library Provision for Researchers* (Anderson Report), HEFCE.

Ollé, J. G. (1967) *Library History*, Bingley.

Research Support Libraries Group (2001) Terms of reference, RSLG. www.rslg.ac.uk/about/terms.asp.

Research Support Libraries Group (2003) *Final Report*. Bristol, Higher Education Funding Council for England, www.rslg.ac.uk/final/final.pdf.

Thompson, J (1977) *A History of the Principles of Librarianship*, Bingley.

University Grants Committee (1921) *Report*, UGC.

University Grants Committee (1967) *Report of the Committee on Libraries* (Parry Report), HMSO.

University Grants Committee (1976) *Report on Capital Provision for University Libraries* (Atkinson Report), HMSO.

Further reading

General information on developments in academic libraries in the UK can be found in the *SCONUL Newsletter* and *CILIP Update*.

3
The library in the institution

Introduction

As has been observed in the first two chapters, academic libraries have many different origins and many different characteristics. They express their missions, aims and objectives in many different ways. However, they share the same - or very similar - purposes and they deliver their services through the same or similar functions. In this chapter the emphasis is on the common characteristics of academic libraries. The key question is: 'What *is* an academic library in the 21st century?' In answering this question, it is essential to look at some of the trends and influences which are moulding libraries at the present time. Of particular importance is the influence of information and communication technologies (ICTs), and it is necessary therefore to look in some detail at how libraries are developing in the ICT-rich environment of the modern university and the modern world.

Perceptions of 'libraries'

Different people have different views of what a 'library' is. To some it is a building, often one of some prominence - for example, the British Library is often thought of in terms of its modern new building at St Pancras, with the other services almost unrecognized. To other people, the 'library' - perhaps the local public library - may be a place to read newspapers and magazines. Others may think of collections of ancient volumes held in an archive. A 'library' may also be a place to ask for information when it is needed. In the workplace it could house company records. Computing professionals have 'libraries' of software. Public perceptions may also be coloured by stereotypes of librarians - all too often a fierce middle-aged woman with glasses and hair in a bun, an image not helped by numerous television depictions!

All of these images (even the last!) have some truth in them, but they are less than helpful in thinking about the purposes of the academic library and why it exists. They mix up ends and means, and they leave unanswered questions about how libraries should develop in a rapidly changing, ICT-intensive world. It is useful, therefore, to consider briefly some rather more systematic ideas about libraries.

The purpose of a library

So, why do we need libraries? What role do they play? As a starting point it is still useful to refer to Ranganathan's 'laws of library science', formulated over 70 years ago in India (Ranganathan, 1931):

- Books are for use
- Every reader his book
- Every book its reader
- Save the time of the reader
- A library is a growing organism

even if the last of these is now rather questionable and the term 'book' needs redefinition.

One of the reasons that Ranganathan's laws are still useful is that they help us to focus on two key aspects of library service. First, that libraries are about what he called 'books' but which today we might broaden out to include all kinds of information and works of creative imagination – 'information objects'. Secondly, and perhaps even more importantly, Ranganathan reminds us that libraries are about people – readers, users, patrons – that it is the *use* of these information objects that is central.

Bearing this in mind, the role of the library may be analysed from a number of perspectives. The traditional approach has been to emphasize collection building and collection management. In essence the library's key task is to build broader and deeper collections and to arrange for users to access those collections only on terms which ensure their long-term integrity. In this view the library is essentially a repository, and most of the activity is devoted to maintenance of that repository. Use can be almost incidental. Figure 3.1 illustrates this.

Figure 3.1 The library as collection

A second approach has been to apply systems concepts, taken from general management theory, and to view the library in terms of resource flows and processes. Buckland (1988) has written extensively on this interpretation which, in its simplest form, is illustrated in Figure 3.2.

Figure 3.2 Systems model

Two important issues arise from this analysis. First, it provides a managerial perspective that recognizes that all the resources which a library absorbs – not just new books and journals, but accommodation, staff, consumables and the rest – have to be managed, that they are interdependent and that they have to be acted upon by processes to produce outputs. A simple example would be a book which is received from the bookseller – an input – then catalogued – a process – and finally lent to a user – an output. Subsequently the user may read the book and become better informed – an outcome. This model suggests that the library must be *active* rather than passive. It also follows that the efficiency of these processes and their relevance to the library's specific aims and objectives are of supreme importance. Secondly, systems approaches focus attention on outcomes and impacts, that is on the difference that the library makes to its users. Users, instead of being incidental, are the raison d'être of the service.

New models of the library

Although these kinds of model are useful to describe a library which is a discrete, independent organization, serving its distinctive user group, it is less obvious that they offer the insights we need when operating within a global, networked information 'space'. For a start, the information resources that the individual library treats as 'inputs' have become far more diverse, and many are not owned by the library but accessed across networks as and when they are required. They might include:

- books published in the traditional way, electronic books and mixed media books in a variety of formats (e.g. paper, CD-ROM)
- journals published in paper, electronic and hybrid formats
- reports, whether paper or electronic or both
- patents, standards, etc whether paper or electronic or both
- official documents, including legislation, again whether paper or electronic or both
- slides and other images in analogue formats
- images in digital formats
- analogue audio tapes
- digital audio
- analogue video
- digital video
- geospatial information, such as paper-based and digital maps
- collections of data, e.g. in demographic databases
- grey literature, such as 'junk' mail, election addresses, etc.
- websites and individual web pages
- computer files of various types
- streamed data, such as that from satellite observation or news-feeds
- semi-published or unpublished company records
- dynamic documents created when they are requested
- dynamic documents updated automatically from a remote source.

It is useful to refer to the total information resources potentially available in the world as the 'information universe'. The sub-set selected by a particular library – recognizing that this sub-set will be changing all the time – is its 'information population'.

But the information population is not all. A library may now have to address a much more diverse and changeable group of users than hitherto. It will include distance learners, those registered for short courses whose membership may last only a few weeks or even less, and those with long-term membership. It may also include members of staff from local companies which pay for membership, members of other local universities and members of the public. Furthermore the rights that members have to access resources may differ – for example, access to an expensive market research data service might be restricted to the MBA students, while access to JISC data services (see Chapter 5) is restricted to members of the university itself. If we regard the total group of all actual and potential users as the 'user universe', which given the co-operative access arrangements now in place may include all academic staff in all UK universities, together with many other groups, we might then term the actual eligible users at any one time the 'user population'. This leads to a symmetric model as shown in Figure 3.3.

User universe	User population	Library	Information population	Information universe

Figure 3.3 User and information populations

Viewed in this way, it becomes appropriate to describe the library as an 'intermediary' or 'broker' between the user and the information resources. The term 'gateway' is also used although it implies a rather passive approach. The role may better be seen as an active one, centred on creating linkages between each individual user and the information resources that user requires, whether or not these resources are owned by and stored in a library. A number of authors have developed this idea of the library further (e.g. Owen and Wiercx (1996), Dempsey, Russell and Murray (1999), Brophy (2001)) and it is particularly applicable to services which are offered in the electronic environment, where the library may be remote from both the user and the information source. However, it is sufficiently broad to be applied to real-world libraries providing both electronic and traditional services.

Hybrid libraries

Despite the rapid development of services based on electronic information, libraries have a continuing role both as stores of books and other physical information objects and as places where people interact with information sources, with information experts and with each other. It is also important to emphasize that all the evidence available would suggest that physical books and journals – print on paper – have a considerable future. The challenge for academic librarians is to manage services which offer users a carefully selected and presented mix of different formats and media. This concept has come to be known as the 'hybrid library' and has been defined as follows:

> The hybrid library was designed to bring a range of technologies from different sources together in the context of a working library, and also to begin to explore integrated systems and services in both the electronic and print environments. The hybrid library should integrate access to all . . . kinds of resources . . . using different technologies from the digital library world, and across different media.   (Rusbridge, 1998)

The concept of the hybrid library recognizes that both 'traditional' (i.e. print-based) and electronic services have advantages, but each also has disadvantages. For example in the traditional model:

1   Each item (book or journal issue – or volume when issues are bound together) can only be used serially (i.e. when one user borrows it, even to use in the library, no-one else can do so until it is returned).
2   Libraries can stock only a small selection of all the items of potential interest to their users.
3   Publication processes involve considerable delays between author, editor, publisher, printer, distributor and library, resulting in material being dated even before it is added to stock.
4   The cost of stocking items that are little used is very high, since staffing and space costs are dominant in this model.
5   There are high costs, especially staffing costs, associated with handling physical objects (e.g. re-shelving, shelf tidying).
6   Heavily used items, such as texts on reading lists, wear out.

The electronic model also has its disadvantages:

1   The quality of information objects – such as whether or not they can be regarded as authoritative, including issues about controlling versions of an object – is often uncertain or simply unknown.

2   Browsing is difficult at the detailed item level, since computer displays are entirely page-oriented. There is no real electronic equivalent to looking through a shelf of books on a particular subject.

3   The economic model is uncertain, resulting in severe restrictions on accessing valuable content where suppliers try to ensure that copies cannot 'leak' into general circulation without their receiving adequate recompense. For a publisher the 'nightmare' scenario is that selling a single copy, which then becomes networked, could represent the total achievable sales of the product.

4   Libraries are frequently able to purchase only a licence to access content; they do not own 'their' copy.

5   There is no consensus on how long-term preservation of electronic information objects can be secured, and there are few provisions for legal deposit.

6   The electronic library is poor at encouraging social interaction, since 'group' study via technology is as yet artificial, limited and generally unattractive.

It therefore seems highly unlikely that the undoubted benefits of the electronic or digital model will enable it to become dominant in the foreseeable future. Not only does the traditional, largely print-based model have several advantages, but there is an enormous investment in 'legacy systems' – content and infrastructure, including systems for publishing content in traditional forms, which have been built up over many years and which retain immense value. For all these reasons, it is likely that for the foreseeable future academic libraries will operate on the hybrid model.

Library services

In succeeding chapters we will examine the range of services offered by academic libraries in some detail, but by way of introduction they are summarized here. It is worth noting that the idea of the library as a *service* – in the sense of the active provider of services to its customers – is relatively new. However, it is now generally accepted that the guiding principle of most academic libraries is the provision of *access* rather than the building of *collections*. (This has sometimes been referred to as the 'access v holdings' debate.) As we will see, among the driving principles for most modern organizations are customer service and customer satisfaction, and libraries are part of this trend. The services that they offer, therefore, are based on a judgement of what their customers need and want.

It is worth noting that the terminology used by libraries to describe their customers varies considerably. At one time *reader* was common, although there was then scope for confusion between human readers and those needed to read microforms! *User* is probably still the preferred term in most academic libraries, although *patron* has crossed the Atlantic - often embedded in an American library management system - and has entered the English vocabulary. Some prefer to use *client*, which has a connotation of a professional relationship - this is discussed further in the next chapter. In this book the term *user* is preferred.

Accepting that libraries are, in the hybrid model, based on collections of information objects which may be held by the library or accessed on behalf of the user from a remote location, the services which surround this core resource will usually include:

1   Catalogues of the stock to which access can be provided. The library's own holdings will usually be presented in an *online public access catalogue* (OPAC), while bibliographies (including web-based lists with clickable links), indexes and abstracts will provide the route to access the collections of other libraries and resources.
2   The delivery of documents to the user in a variety of ways. This includes the loan of books and other items whether from stock or via interlibrary loan, the facility to use items for reference and the provision of copies of both printed and electronic documents to the user.
3   Space suitable for study purposes, with a series of ancillary services such as access to a PC, photocopying, light boxes for slides, and microform readers and reader-printers. As we shall see in Chapter 9, a variety of study spaces is needed.
4   Advisory services, able to answer a range of different types of query, from directional enquiries - such as the location of particular stock - to complex information questions requiring detailed subject knowledge and familiarity with specialized information sources. The library will also frequently be seen as the centre of expertise on such matters as copyright.

5   Support services, which may be targeted at academic departments, designed to provide a broad range of support to specific courses or to research programmes. The actual services delivered may be tailored to particular requirements, as with a current awareness service for researchers or a collection of readings for an undergraduate course.

6   Skills development, particularly services designed to enable students to develop the information skills they need to study effectively, and those which will enable them to be effective in later employment.

7   Other services, determined by the local library. For example, many academic libraries hold valuable archive collections and will provide a comprehensive service to enable scholars to access and use them as well as undertaking conservation work.

Information strategies

We saw in Chapter 2 that one of the recommendations of the Follett Committee was that institutions should develop information strategies. In 1995, JISC issued guidelines to institutions on how information strategies should be prepared and the broad issues they should address (JISC, 1995) – the introduction spoke of information as the 'life blood of higher education institutions'. This advice made it clear that the issue was one of organizing and managing the total information resources of the institution, regardless of whether they were generated internally or externally, and whether or not they were generated and accessed using information and communications technologies. The work was heavily influenced both by the concept of information resource management, which has its roots in information science, and by that of knowledge management, which has become a dominant issue in the corporate sector. The development of JISC's information strategy initiative was described by Brindley (1998), who was one of its chief architects, and the initiative received further support within the recommendations of the Dearing Report (see Chapter 1). JISC updated its advice to institutions in 1998 (JISC, 1998).

For a number of years thereafter, JISC worked with a selected group of universities to explore how information strategies which truly influenced practice could best be developed. Latterly, however, responsibility for this work has largely been devolved to the JISC 'InfoNET' which, based at the University of Northumbria, operates under the strapline 'Providing

Expertise in Planning and Implementing Information Systems'. In many ways this seems to have been a backwards step: most of InfoNET's advice is at the management, not the strategic level, and is concerned with the procurement and implementation of individual systems – the use of 'systems' rather than 'strategies' is telling. InfoNET provides a source for information strategy case study reports (www.jiscinfonet.ac.uk/Resources/saved-searches/info-strategy-case-studies) but, as of late 2004, it had not provided revised advice on information strategies as such in its 'Infokits' service.

Convergence

As academic libraries have become more dependent on the use of computers for the delivery of so many of their services, their relationships with their institutions' computing services has become much closer. IT has also become much more embedded in learning, for students are commonly required to word process their assignments and may be required to use spreadsheets, databases and other software and will frequently undertake part of their studies through a Virtual Learning Environment (VLE – see Chapter 10). The library has proved to be the obvious, central location to house large numbers of workstations, and many libraries have built extensions precisely for this purpose. From the user's point of view it has also been unhelpful to have two separate sources of advice on problems related to the use of electronic information services. It is not unknown for a user to approach the library help desk with a problem with using a particular package only to be told that it is an 'IT problem' and he or she must go to the computer centre for advice. Having gone across campus to the computer centre, and possibly queued at the help desk there, the user is now told that it is a 'library' problem! For the user, a unified service makes a great deal of sense. From the point of view of institutional management, there are also attractions in bringing the two services together under one manager enabling IT provision to be co-ordinated. There may also be savings in management and other staffing costs.

For these reasons a trend towards the *convergence* of library and computer services in British higher and further education institutions started during the 1990s. As a result many librarians now work in converged services alongside colleagues with a computing background. A distinction needs to be drawn between *operational* convergence, where the two services work closely together, perhaps under the direction of a single senior manager, and *organizational* convergence, where the two services are effectively merged into one.

The extent to which organizational convergence can be achieved is still open to question and there has certainly been a slackening in the pace of convergence in recent years. For example, some would argue that the enquiry service can be fully converged with front-line staff dealing with any 'library' or 'computing' questions that arise, passing them on to experts when necessary. Others would contend that the span of knowledge needed to understand the full range of questions, from software problems to the use of manuscripts, is too wide to be handled effectively by the same set of staff. Day et al. (1996) suggested that the factors which help to achieve smooth convergence of services include:

- encouragement to converge operations as overlaps are identified
- good horizontal (i.e. between peers) and vertical (i.e. between staff at different levels) communications
- joint staff training and development in order to promote shared understanding of different cultures and viewpoints
- specific training for staff involved in change, and management support for them
- identification of key post holders who can act as 'change agents' – people who will champion change and take a positive attitude to it
- leadership and clear direction from management
- IT and information strategies which are linked into the institution's strategic goals.

Particular issues may be raised where an academic library operates, as many do, across multiple sites. Here convergence may be given extra impetus by the need to provide IT support to relatively small groups of users at a time when end-user IT access is essential to learning, teaching and research.

Library co-operation

There is a long tradition of co-operation between libraries in the UK, although only in recent years have academic libraries come to see co-operative approaches to service delivery as an essential part of their provision. One of the reasons for this is that, unlike other developed countries, the majority of interlibrary lending has been centralized through the British Library's Document Supply Services with other academic libraries acting only as back-up resources. In addition, during the expansion of higher education from the late 1960s to the mid-1990s, some older university libraries took a very protectionist stance against allowing access to anyone not a registered student or member of staff of their institution. For a variety of reasons these barriers started to come down during the 1990s and this trend has continued. Librarians recognize that no academic library can claim to be self-sufficient and the benefits of co-operative approaches are therefore being examined carefully.

A number of consortia have developed which agree to provide common access and sometimes borrowing rights to those in membership of any of the constituent libraries. For example, the North West Academic Libraries (NoWAL) consortium has an agreement that all staff may borrow from any of the libraries and that students may have access for reference purposes. The M25 scheme in London covers a much larger number of libraries and operates similar, though more limited, agreements.

In 1999 the *UK Libraries Plus* scheme was launched, enabling part-time, distance and placement students to borrow from libraries in their home or work area, with provision for staff and full-time students to use other libraries for reference purposes (UK Libraries Plus, 2004). The scheme does not extend to electronic materials, partly because of complexities over licensing, but of course many such materials can be accessed directly under arrangements made by the home library.

Conclusion

Libraries are changing. The old models, based on the idea of a library as a storehouse of knowledge, are giving way to concepts based on the development of 'intermediary' roles, acted out in a hybrid environment in which resources may be in either traditional or electronic formats. To deliver services within such scenarios requires new forms of organization, perhaps through convergence with IT departments or with those responsible for designing learning environments, and will certainly require a high degree of co-operation and co-ordination between libraries and other agencies. Librarians will need to be very clear about the purposes that their libraries serve, and will need to design the range of services they offer with those purposes in mind. It may be that those services will be very different from the ones to which they and their users have been accustomed.

References

Brindley, L. (1998) Information Strategies. In Hanson, T. and Day, J. (eds), *Managing the Electronic Library: a practical guide for information professionals*, Bowker-Saur, 27–48.

Brophy, P. (2001) *The Library in the Twenty-first Century*, London, Facet Publishing.

Buckland, M. K. (1988) *Library Services in Theory and Practice*, Pergamon Press, 2nd edn.

Day, J. M. et al. (1996) Higher Education, Teaching, Learning and the Electronic Library: a review of the literature for the IMPEL2 project: monitoring organisational and cultural change, *The New Review of Academic Librarianship*, **2**, 131–204.

Dempsey, L., Russell, R. and Murray, R. (1999) Utopian Place of Criticism? Brokering access to network information, *Journal of Documentation*, **55** (1), 33–70.

Joint Information Systems Committee (1995) *Guidelines for Developing an Information Strategy*, JISC.

Joint Information Systems Committee (1998) *Guidelines for Developing an Information Strategy: the sequel*, JISC.

Owen, J. S. M. and Wiercx, A. (1996) *Knowledge Models for Networked Library Services: final report*, Report PROLIB/KMS 16905, Office of Official Publications of the European Communities.

Ranganathan, S. R. (1931) *Five Laws of Library Science*, Madras Library Association.

Rusbridge, C. (1998) Towards the Hybrid Library, *D-Lib Magazine*, July–August, www.dlib.org/dlib/july98/rusbridge/07rusbridge.html.

UK Libraries Plus (2004), www.uklibrariesplus.ac.uk/.

Further reading

Information on current policy developments in UK higher education libraries can be found on the funding councils area of the HERO service

www.hero.ac.uk/uk/home/index.cfm

on the SCONUL website (where the quarterly *SCONUL Focus* can be downloaded)

www.sconul.ac.uk

and on the UKOLN website

www.ukoln.ac.uk/

4

Users of the academic library

Introduction

As we saw in Chapter 3, without users there is little point in having a
library. This is true even of those libraries which have as their primary
mission the preservation of recorded knowledge for posterity, for unless
'posterity' includes users it has no real meaning. In this chapter we will look
at the major groups of users which the academic library serves and consider
how truly user-centred services can be developed.

Because libraries are *services*, they exist to provide a service to people
who need it. The service may be the provision of access to textbooks, or
assistance with information enquiries, or the provision of a place to study,
or help with using a complex computer-based information retrieval
package, but it is always the user on whom such activities are focused. It
is important for librarians to continually re-examine whether their services
are still providing what users want and need.

To help answer this question, and then to provide suitable management
and service responses, it is useful to borrow the techniques of quality
management, developed in the industrial and commercial sectors but now
widely implemented throughout public services. Fundamental to quality
management is the understanding that quality is inextricably linked to
customer satisfaction. Indeed the two classic definitions of quality which
are most widely accepted are:

> Quality is conformance to the customer's requirements

and

> Quality is fitness for the customer's purposes.

Both of these definitions emphasize that the customer - or, in the more usual library terminology, 'user' - is the focus of judgements about quality. Quality management is considered in greater detail in Chapter 12 within the context of overall management issues. However, before making any assumptions about the needs, wants and preferences of library users, it is important to clarify just who those users are.

Who are the users?

Although the immediate answer to this question may appear to be 'staff and students of the institution', it is more useful to take a broad view of the idea of the 'user' and borrow terminology from general management. Modern approaches, which are exemplified in the literature on quality management, suggest that the idea of *stakeholders* provides the most useful approach, using the idea that there are many groups of people who have a legitimate interest in what the organization - in this case, the library - does. The European Foundation for Quality Management (EFQM) has a model of 'business excellence' which it uses in assessing entrants for its European Quality Award and half of the assessment is based on what are called 'results' - yet prominent among these are the effect of the organization on its environment and the satisfaction of the people who work for it (EFQM, 2000). Bearing in mind that higher and further education institutions are working in the public sector, where much of their responsibility is to society as a whole, a broad view of the academic library's stakeholders might include:

- undergraduate students
- postgraduate taught students
- postgraduate research students
- teaching staff
- research staff
- university management, including, for example, heads of academic departments as well as senior management
- former students (called 'alumni')
- members of the local business community
- members of the local public (including organized community groups)
- the higher education funding councils (which provide much of the funding and expect accountability for it)

- the government, through the Department for Education and Skills and the Department for Culture, Media and Sport in England and Wales, the Scottish Executive in Scotland and the Secretary of State in Northern Ireland
- the local or regional library community, including specialized and public libraries and other academic libraries which rely on co-operative agreements
- the national and international research community, especially in relation to special collections or services
- the national and international library community, especially in relation to interlibrary loan and other co-operative arrangements
- the library and information professions
- posterity – future users of materials which are currently being added to stock.

The librarian must balance the needs of each of these groups, bearing in mind that their views on what makes a good library service will differ markedly. An interesting study carried out by a research team at Glasgow Caledonian University in the mid-1990s showed that, when asked to suggest how the performance of an academic library might best be measured, different stakeholder groups came up with very different answers (Pickering, Crawford and McLelland, 1996). Senior institutional managers suggested that the best measure would be 'the competence of library managers'; part-time undergraduates chose 'the number of multiple copies of popular books provided'; research staff chose 'staff helpfulness', which was also chosen by junior library staff; while senior library staff thought it was the 'ease of use of the OPAC', presumably since this is the entry point to so many other services.

Balancing these viewpoints is by no means an easy task, especially as the demands of one group of users may conflict with those of others. In the following sections, we will look at some of the characteristics of the major groups.

Undergraduate students

Undergraduate students form the largest user group of most universities, although there are some, such as Cranfield, which specialize in postgraduate work. In the past, undergraduates were sometimes assumed to be a fairly homogeneous group. The traditional undergraduate had progressed to university from school at age 18, was studying full-time on a traditionally designed course (lectures, tutorials, assignments, reading lists etc.), had good basic academic skills (to 'A' level) and received regular tutorials from academic staff. The development of mass higher education and efforts to widen participation have destroyed any validity that this picture ever had. Now the library must assume that many undergraduates will be mature (i.e. over 25), many will be part-time, fitting study alongside work and family responsibilities, many will have non-traditional qualifications which have less 'academic' content than 'A' levels and many will have difficulty adjusting to the culture of higher education.

It is not surprising that in these circumstances the needs of undergraduate students are often quite difficult to assess, although it is notable that in most studies carried out even in the early years of this century the over-riding concern of undergraduate students was for an adequate supply of textbooks and other recommended reading. In other words, their requirements for information sources are highly directed and for much of their studies, certainly in the earlier years, go little further than the reading lists issued to them. This may also be particularly true of part-time students who have little time to explore the literature more fully. Conversely, however, final year undergraduates are now commonly required to undertake an extended project, so at this stage they may turn suddenly from a highly directed mode of library use to an exploratory mode, frequently encountering significant difficulties in so doing. This may therefore be the stage at which library information skills training, as discussed later in this chapter, is most effective.

For the library manager this creates a number of issues, not least that with highly structured delivery it is likely that all students in a class will descend on the library at the same time to demand the same book. With large class sizes (and over 100 students to a class is not uncommon) this creates an immediate problem. The library cannot stock one copy for every student (and probably should not, since to do so would reduce the budget available to purchase a wide range of sources), so it needs to find ways of sharing out a limited number of copies fairly. The usual answer to this is to operate a short-loan collection (see Chapter 11) although services offering 'electronic short loan' or ebooks are becoming available (see Chapter 5).

Issues which need to be considered include whether the library *should* be supplying this book if it is *required* reading: was the tutor's intention that students should purchase their own copies? With increasing financial pressures on students, there has undoubtedly been a shift of expectation towards library supply, but is this reasonable? Would it be better for the library to hold a limited number of reference copies?

Full-time undergraduates may view the library as the main place where they can study, although this will depend on other factors such as the proximity of their accommodation and its suitability and the availability of electronic resources accessible from off campus. It will also be likely that some groups of undergraduates will be less likely to use the library for study than others. For example, mature students with family responsibilities may not have the time to spend on campus, while part-time students – especially those studying in the evenings – may not have the opportunity. Some academic libraries have developed specific services to try to meet the needs of these non-traditional groups. For example, weekend opening has become more common, collections of textbooks earmarked for loan only to part-time students have been introduced and document delivery services which accept requests from home or work and deliver in the same way have been established. Some libraries have designated a specific member of staff to take responsibility for services to part-time students and to act as a point of contact with them.

Where undergraduates use the library as a place to study, they will expect a range of services to be available. Most obviously they will want study space, and it needs to be remembered that while some people need a quiet environment in which to study, others prefer some noise and some may need to work as a group (see Chapter 9 for the implications of this for library building design). Some study spaces will need to be equipped with workstations, but others will need to be suitable for the use of printed materials – and many users of course will want flexible spaces suitable for both. Undergraduates are also likely to be heavy users of reference and enquiry services.

Students make a great deal of use of photocopying facilities – to the extent that it sometimes appears that photocopying is a substitute for reading! Obviously they will also use the range of standard services, as described in Chapter 3.

Undergraduate students often lack the basic skills to make good use of libraries and it should not be forgotten that many, particularly younger, students will never before have encountered a library on the scale of the typical university library. If their experience is of school libraries, they will need to acquire a number of new skills quickly in order to be effective users and in particular will need to come to grips with the sheer range of resources at their disposal. The issue of information skills is discussed later in this chapter, but it should be noted that first impressions are particularly important. Some academic libraries have used staff as 'greeters' in the first few weeks of the academic year to give new students a warm welcome and to help them make their first use of the library. Induction tours are common, and these can be followed up later by more intensive training organized on a subject basis.

Postgraduate students

It is to be hoped that postgraduates will have previous experience of using an academic library, although this will not always be the case as postgraduate courses vary considerably. As noted in Chapter 1, while some are effectively *conversion* courses which introduce students to a new area, and thus have much in common with the final year of an undergraduate degree, others are *end-on* courses, which extend the students' knowledge and skills gained in their degree studies. These latter courses may be taken by students immediately after their first degree, or they may be a continuing development course taken later to update and modernize skills and knowledge. Postgraduate students are also, on average, older than undergraduates and are more likely to have experience of the world of work.

Although some courses will rely heavily on reading lists, it is much more likely that postgraduate students will be required to 'read around' their subject, finding sources of information for themselves. Postgraduates are also more likely to be concerned with the latest advances in their field. For these reasons they are likely to want to make considerable use of the periodical literature and they will need to explore abstracts and indexes to identify items of interest, some of which may need to be supplied by interlibrary loan if they are not available electronically. In addition, postgraduate students may make different demands on the library for study space as, depending on the structure of their courses, they may be engaged in individual or group study and the types of spaces they need will depend on this.

Research students and staff

Postgraduate research students will usually be undertaking an MPhil (Master of Philosophy) or PhD (Doctor of Philosophy) programme or its equivalent. Although these programmes require the student to undertake individual, original research they usually also include a taught element, particularly to cover research methods. It is helpful if the library has an input to this element to ensure that library support can be fully explained and advanced information skills developed.

In addition to research students, universities employ research assistants and research fellows, usually on fixed-term contracts associated with a particular externally funded research project or assisting senior academic staff in their research. The needs of all these users will be similar. Because their research is original, and presumably at the leading edge of developments in their field, the library requirement is for in-depth coverage of a highly specialist area and timeliness is usually of the essence – so, for example, rapid supply of interlibrary loans is important. In other words, they are highly demanding library users. They will certainly want to access a range of electronic resources, such as specialist databases and datasets, and may require original materials which are comparatively rare and difficult to locate. In the arts and humanities, their research may be based on specialist library collections and archives (see Chapter 11).

Of course these users also want the standard library services: photocopying, lending, and so on. They may also require rather more specialized study space than others, especially if they do not have adequate space in their departments. They may also place heavy demands on interlibrary loan services, although where externally funded they may be more willing to pay for this from their research grants than others would be.

Academic staff

Most staff in universities have both teaching and research responsibilities, although the balance between these may vary markedly. Although teaching and research will be closely related, and the results of research will be used to inform teaching in the subject, staff may differ in their requirements of the library.

For teaching there may be a spectrum of library support ranging on the one hand from the checking of reading lists to, on the other, close involvement of library staff in the actual delivery of the course. With the development of new teaching and learning methods, and increasing use of ICTs to deliver teaching, the demands on the library are changing. This issue, in the context of the *learning environment* as a whole, is considered further in Chapter 14.

Academic libraries commonly request reading lists from teaching staff well in advance of the start of the course, to allow time for them to be checked, books to be ordered and processed and changes made to the loan status, for example by transferring copies into the short loan collection. However, librarians do not always recognize the constraints under which teaching staff work. With modular courses in particular, staff may not be sure what they will be teaching until a few weeks before the start of the session and in any case requests sent out in the middle of the examination season are hardly likely to receive priority attention. It is important that there is a dialogue between the two sides so that, with understanding of each other's problems, there may be effective action to ensure that the students will be able to access the resources they need when they need them.

The needs of staff for library support for their research will be similar to the requirements of research students and staff, although of course as experts in their field academic staff will be even more demanding. They may value current awareness and alerting services and they will appreciate the availability of co-operative agreements which enable them to use a broader range of collections. National developments, such as the Research Libraries Network (RLN), discussed in Chapter 2, will be welcomed. The role of the specialist subject librarian (see Chapter 6) is of great importance.

External readers

Although few academic libraries have a large body of external readers, apart from where the library attracts significant numbers of researchers to its specialist collections, this group can be important. Those academic libraries with major collections can find themselves under considerable pressure from this direction, and steps have been taken to fund this additional work nationally as a result of the Anderson and RSLG Reports (see Chapter 2).

Other external readers, for example from local businesses – and especially those which are information based, such as legal practices – may be attracted to use the resources and expertise that the library can offer. Another area which has seen considerable growth is the offering of services to client groups which are loosely associated with the institution. The primary example of this derives from the relationship between universities with medical or health-related disciplines and the National Health Service, with heavy demand on libraries to support evidence-based practice. Services to such groups will normally be offered at a fee. The fee itself may be set on an individual basis or may be a group fee (for example, to cover all nurses working within a particular NHS Trust). However, a major source of problems arises when the university itself negotiates a contract with the NHS which includes, but does not specify in detail, the provision of library services. Wherever possible a clear contract which states what the library will and will not provide should be signed. The best practice is to put in place a service level agreement (SLA) and to ensure that monitoring of activity is implemented. The SLA should include a complaints or non-compliance procedure so that both sides know what avenues are open if they are dissatisfied – on the user side with the service, on the library side with compliance with terms (for example, if the users are persistently not returning books they have borrowed). Because the agreement is a legal contract, it should be checked by the university's legal advisers.

Distance learners

In recent years many more institutions have become involved in distance education, particularly at postgraduate level. The support of distance learners can be a major problem for libraries, although there is considerable experience of this and some institutions (such as Sheffield Hallam University) can offer a good exemplar of supporting students at a distance, including the provision of special library services. Bolton, Unwin and Stephens (1998) undertook extensive research into the experiences of postgraduate students with library services in the UK, and found many stories of frustration caused by lack of communication and planning.

The key to providing effective library support to distance learners undoubtedly lies in good forward planning and liaison. Too often a distance learning course is launched with the unwritten expectation that students will be able to find their own library support. While the availability of electronic resources has eased the problem somewhat it is still not unknown for the home institution's library to be unaware that the course has been launched until one of the students telephones to ask for books or other services to be delivered. In the student's home area, the local university may receive a visit from the student who expects to receive the same services as if he or she was a registered student at that institution – and is somewhat put out to find that services are not available, or only on payment of a fee or that arrangements should have been made in advance. Although attempts have been made to improve liaison between libraries – including the excellent UK Libraries Plus scheme described in Chapter 3 – this does not obviate the need for a planned approach.

The situation with franchised courses (where a university course is delivered through a local college) tends to be rather better, since part of the validation procedure consists of checking the adequacy of learning resources. However, the relationship between the institutions involved varies widely. In some, all responsibility rests – sometimes rather unrealistically – on the college. For others, the franchising university assumes some responsibility for back-up library services – the best example of this is the *Virtual Academic Library of the North-West* (VALNOW) service offered by the University of Central Lancashire Library, from its main campus in Preston, to franchise course students throughout Lancashire, Cumbria and beyond.

Users with special needs

It must not be assumed that all users can access services in the same way. Many people require assistance or special consideration if services are to be accessible to them. For example, users may have a visual impairment, may be deaf, may have a motor impairment or may suffer from dyslexia. The 1995 Disability Discrimination Act requires those providing services to take account of such needs and to respond accordingly. More specifically, the Special Educational Needs and Disability Act 2001 (SENDA) gave students with disabilities the right not to be discriminated against in education, including its support services. The general interpretation of SENDA is that a proactive approach is needed: it is not enough simply to wait for discrimination to be highlighted and then deal with it.

Making library services accessible is important because they form such a vital part of the overall service to any member of the university, and careful consideration is therefore needed when services are designed or changed. Further consideration of these issues will be found in Chapter 11.

Measuring user satisfaction

Bearing in mind the number of different user groups and the different perspectives of each, it is clearly important for the library manager to balance demands and to be aware of where problems are occurring. Having up-to-date knowledge of whether users are satisfied with the services being delivered is essential. There are a number of ways in which this can be done and, as we shall see in Chapter 12, the data collected will form an important part of the manager's overall measurement of the library's performance. As well as using specific surveys which ask users directly about their satisfaction, there are a number of other ways in which the views of users and their level of satisfaction can be judged:

1   Many academic libraries have formal library committees, which advise the librarian on policy, with the membership usually being predominantly of users, including student representatives.
2   Less formal groups, often called user groups, may exist or may be formed. Sometimes these may cover all library services; sometimes they will be specific to particular subjects or faculties.
3   Staff can be encouraged to keep a note of problems or informal complaints which users make, preferably through a semi-formal process that ensures that such information is consistently brought to the attention of the appropriate managers – but without pretending that every minor comment should be handled as a major crisis!
4   There should be a formal complaints procedure, preferably accompanied by clear procedures for responding to the complainant, for ensuring that the manager takes the complaint seriously (which is not to say that users are always right!) and for aggregating complaints into a regular report to senior managers.

5   One aspect of the ongoing liaison between the library staff and groups of users, such as academic departments, should be the monitoring of the users' satisfaction.

6   Performance statistics (see Chapter 12) should be monitored for warning signals that may indicate problem areas. For example, is the average time to supply interlibrary loans within acceptable limits?

7   As outlined in Chapter 1, the formal quality audit and quality assurance processes to which all institutions are subject consider learning resources, including library services, and provide a useful source of customer satisfaction data.

8   Finally, where a problem area is identified – or even simply anticipated – it may be useful to draw together an ad hoc group of users – perhaps using focus group techniques – to consider its impact.

As well as considering all these sources of information, it is most important that senior managers maintain excellent contacts throughout the institution, so that they pick up the sometimes quite subtle clues that tell them that a problem may be occurring. Some of this involvement will come about through formal committee meetings and other institutional decision-making bodies; some will come about through informal contacts – walking the corridors and joining colleagues for lunch or coffee. Equally important is keeping close contact with the staff who are at the front-line of service delivery. They will know only too well what the problems are and they need to be encouraged to bring them forward and assured that they will be addressed.

Information skills

It was noted in Chapter 1 that an area on which the Dearing Committee concentrated its recommendations was the need for students to develop *key skills*, including communication skills, numeracy, the use of IT and 'learning how to learn'. Academic libraries have been concerned for many years to help students – and for that matter staff – to develop a broad range of 'information skills'. These should be understood as covering a much wider skills range than IT skills, although they would not cover all the areas identified as key skills by Dearing.

Considerable work has been undertaken in the UK in recent years, under the aegis of SCONUL, to define what is meant by information skills in higher education and to review good practice both in the UK and further afield. In December 1999 SCONUL published an influential briefing paper on this subject which drew attention to the need to distinguish between skills required by students to enable them to study effectively - sometimes called 'study skills' - and those required to enable them to function effectively in the real world where information itself is increasingly the dominant resource (Standing Conference of National and University Libraries, 1999). More recently it has defined information literacy in the following terms: 'information literacy encompasses library user education, information skills training and education, and those areas of personal, transferable or "key" skills relating to the use and manipulation of information in the context of learning, teaching and research issues in higher education' (Standing Conference of National and University Libraries, 2003).

The briefing paper identified seven 'Pillars of Information Literacy', as follows:

1   The ability to recognise a need for information.
2   The ability to distinguish ways in which the information 'gap' may be addressed.
   • Knowledge of appropriate kinds of resources, both print and non-print.
   • Selection of resources with 'best fit' for task at hand.
   • The ability to understand the issues affecting accessibility of sources.
3   The ability to construct strategies for locating information.
   • To articulate information need to match against resources.
   • To develop a systematic method appropriate for the need.
   • To understand the principles of construction and generation of databases.
4   The ability to locate and access information.
   • To develop appropriate searching techniques (e.g. use of Boolean searching).
   • To use communication and information technologies, including international academic networks.
   • To use abstracting and indexing services, citation indexes and databases.

- To use current awareness methods to keep up to date.
5   The ability to compare and evaluate information obtained from different sources.
   - Awareness of bias and authority issues.
   - Awareness of the peer review process of scholarly publishing.
   - Appropriate extraction of information matching the information need.
6   The ability to organise, apply and communicate information to others in ways appropriate to the situation.
   - To cite bibliographic references in project reports and theses.
   - To construct a personal bibliographic system.
   - To apply information to the problem at hand.
   - To communicate effectively using the appropriate medium.
   - To understand issues of copyright and plagiarism.
7   The ability to synthesise and build upon existing information, contributing to the creation of new knowledge.

A major issue for academic librarians is the extent to which information skills tuition should be embedded in the curriculum. There is considerable evidence that this kind of learning is much better absorbed and applied when students can see its relevance to their immediate needs. So, for example, learning how to search complex datasets is relevant when an assignment requiring the identification of relevant sources from across the subject's literature is required – it is likely that relevant information skills training will be much better received at this stage than if given in a vacuum at the start of the course. The success of information skills tuition will depend on the development of good working relationships between librarians and teaching staff, so that appropriate tuition can be planned into course delivery from the start. The need for good working relationships and indeed partnership between library and academic staff is a topic that will be considered further in Chapter 6.

Conclusion

Libraries exist to serve their users, but the user population is increasingly heterogeneous. The days when the academic library could assume that its users were either scholars pursuing their research and teaching interests or full-time undergraduates straight from school have vanished. Today's user may be full- or part-time, may be studying at a distance, perhaps on a course franchised to a local college, may be pursuing funded research as part of an international team or may be a part-time teacher brought in to lead a specific module. Many students are mature, with wide work experience and very different expectations from those of their counterparts only a few decades ago. In seeking to provide appropriate services, it is essential that the needs of all the different users are taken into account and that the library plays its part, by providing opportunities for the development of information skills, in enabling all users to make the most of their interactions with information resources.

References

Bolton, N., Unwin, L. and Stephens, K. (1998) *The Role of the Library in Distance Learning: a study of postgraduate students, course providers and librarians in the UK*, Bowker-Saur.

European Foundation for Quality Management (2000) *The EFQM Excellence Model* and *European Quality Awards*, www.efqm.org/.

Pickering, H., Crawford, J. C. and McLelland, D. (1996) *The Stakeholder Approach to the Construction of Performance Measures*, Glasgow Caledonian University.

Standing Conference of National and University Libraries (1999) *Information Skills in Higher Education*, SCONUL,
www.sconul.ac.uk/activities/inf_lit/papers/Seven_pillars.html.

Standing Conference of National and University Libraries (2003) *Information Literacy*. SCONUL,
www.sconul.ac.uk/activities/inf_lit/About_us.html.

Further reading

Brophy, P. and Coulling, K. (1996) *Quality Management for Information & Library Managers*, Gower.

5

The impacts and opportunities of information and communications technologies

Introduction

Of all the influences on academic libraries, there can be no doubt that the development of information and communications technologies (ICTs) has been the most important and the most far-reaching in living memory. We have already seen that considerations of management and user focus have led to a trend of convergence between computing and library services in academic institutions. Although there has been some reaction against this, no-one is seriously suggesting that the academic library of the future will be anything but dependent on ICTs both for delivery of services and for much (some would even say all) of its information content.

In this chapter we consider first of all what the significant ICTs are, and then examine the ways in which academic libraries have been exploiting the opportunities which they offer. In Chapter 8 we will examine some of the actual content - bibliographic services, electronic journals, and so on - which are available to academic users. Then in Chapter 10 we examine the library's computer-based management systems and related issues.

Digital content

We saw in Chapter 3 that the range of resources which are the 'stuff' of academic libraries - the information universe - has grown enormously, not just in volume but also in kind. Where libraries in the past dealt predominantly with printed books and journals, having limited collections of newer media such as slides, audio and video tapes, they now find that a very significant proportion of their materials are electronic: digitized data, text, audio, video and multimedia files.

In the early 1970s academic libraries began to use commercial database systems, such as the medical bibliographic database MEDLINE to provide a specialist service to individual researchers. In addition to the provision of one-off searching, various experiments were carried out with selective dissemination of information (SDI) systems, which were designed to match the 'profile' of a user's interests against each update of the database to provide a list of current references. Access to these information retrieval systems was almost invariably charged on a *connect time* or *number of hits* basis, or a combination of the two, and most were by no means easy to use. As a result the norm during this period – up to the early 1990s – was for *mediated searching*: a trained librarian would perform the searches either with the user sitting alongside or on the basis of a user's expressed needs. Costs meant that the service had to be restricted – usually to academic staff and researchers – and often it was available only by appointment. An important skill was the ability to keep costs down by searching quickly and effectively. The facility to formulate searches offline and then to go online only to execute them became a selling-point for these systems.

At the beginning of the 1990s, new services based on digitization of full text started to become widely available. Among the pioneers was Aston University Library, which in 1992-3 installed the ADONIS biomedical periodical service. Based on full text of approximately 500 biomedical journals held on CD-ROMs in a juke-box, this system allowed the university to offer access via a library workstation to a large volume of journal literature: the system was later networked across campus, though initially requests had to be sent to the library, which printed off the requested paper and mailed it to the user!

To compare this situation with that which pertains now is to recognize how far libraries have travelled in a very short space of time. The norm now is for end-user access to full text, and users independently access vast information resources across the internet, using the world wide web (WWW) as the medium for delivery. Some have even asked why we still need libraries. The answer to that question lies partly in the continued importance of some printed resources, partly in the additional services that libraries provide and partly, as we saw in Chapter 3, in their role as intermediaries – selecting the highest quality sources, ensuring that the most up-to-date sources are available, and making them all easily accessible. How technology enables them to achieve the latter task is the subject of this chapter.

The infrastructure for information delivery

Before effective use of digital content can be contemplated it is essential to have in place an adequate infrastructure to deliver that content: the 'pipes' of the electronic 'plumbing'. It is convenient to think of these requirements as being in two parts: the internal, local area networks of the institution itself, and the regional, national and international infrastructure which enables remote sources to be accessed and services to be delivered to remote users. Coupled with this is the computing power to exploit the digital content: servers to run databases and other applications and end-user workstations to provide the manipulation and display of data at the desktop. Already the 1980s had seen massive changes in this area: servers had become relatively cheap, and it was certainly possible for an academic library to install a server with enough power to run library applications at reasonable cost by the early 1990s. Of far more importance, however, was the availability of affordable workstations: networked PCs (and to a much lesser extent Apple Macs) provided the desktop connections and computing power needed.

For libraries to take on their new role as information intermediaries it was essential that their institutions had adequate internal infrastructures. This was not achieved overnight, but it was noticeable that within the institution it was often the library which led the way in installing the necessary, initially fairly crude, infrastructure. The reason for this is that libraries actually had content which was worth delivering across networks, while other potential users had not yet determined how the networks should be used. Among the first applications to be networked in this way was the library catalogue, which rapidly became known as the *Online Public Access Catalogue* (OPAC).

Externally, the key development in the UK was the implementation of the Joint Academic Network (JANET). A development from the regional computing centres which had been established when large computers were too expensive for any one institution to justify, JANET was an ambitious project to provide high-speed network connections between all UK universities. Libraries became significant users of this service, not least through the establishment of the Bath Information and Data Services (BIDS) service at the University of Bath, providing the whole HE community with access to the Institute for Scientific Information (ISI) datasets (*Science Citation Index* and the other citation indexes). This development itself was enabled through the Joint Information Systems Committee (JISC) which was set up by the four higher education funding councils. JISC established the Information Services Sub-Committee (ISSC) to oversee the purchase and mounting of such datasets. A key principle, and one that proved vital to the huge success of these initiatives, was that access must be *free at the point of use* – in other words the student or member of staff must not be charged for accessing the service. Instead the service would be paid for by a mix of JISC funding (in effect top-slicing of university budgets to provide national services) and institutional subscriptions. Limiting the time a user spent online or the number of citations retrieved was abandoned. Mediated searching was no longer necessary on cost grounds and users started to become familiar with searching databases for themselves.

During the 1990s, JISC supported the establishment of three *data centres*: BIDS at the University of Bath, the Manchester Information and Associated Services (MIMAS, formerly MIDAS) at the University of Manchester and Edinburgh Data and INformation Access (EDINA) at the University of Edinburgh. In addition there are a number of more specialist services which serve the academic community as a whole. Between them these centres hosted the servers and databases to which UK higher education had negotiated access.

The Follett Report

In Chapter 2 the background to the establishment of the Follett Committee was described and it was noted that one of the key areas it examined, and the focus of many of its recommendations, was the use of IT. In the event, these recommendations were rapidly adopted by the funding councils and the Follett Implementation Group for Information Technology (with the memorable acronym of FIGIT) was set up to plan and oversee implementation. Working closely with the ISSC, the decision was made to establish the *Electronic Libraries Programme* (eLib). This is described in some detail in the next section.

At the same time, the Follett Report's recommendations on the funding of new and refurbished buildings, although directed primarily at easing the library space problem, had the effect of providing opportunities for higher education libraries to be equipped with the latest networking technology and with study spaces designed to take computer workstations. In other words libraries found themselves in the fortunate position of being able to acquire:

- local infrastructure suited to the delivery of electronic services
- connections to a high speed, dedicated academic network
- a rapidly increasing selection of electronic datasets, most of which were housed at national centres so that libraries did not have to concern themselves with the problem of mounting and maintaining them
- a programme of development geared to the production of new, relevant services, again funded nationally.

It is no exaggeration to state that this combination of factors placed UK higher education libraries in a unique position to exploit the opportunities of the information revolution.

Before turning to examine eLib in detail, however, it is worth noting some other developments which were taking place at the same time in this area. These included:

- The adoption of CD-ROM based databases by libraries, leading fairly rapidly to the implementation of CD-ROM networks – at first these were standalone networks (i.e. not connected to anything else) but they then evolved to become part of the library and then campus network.
- The European Commission Telematics for Libraries Programme, which enabled a considerable number of large-scale international research and development projects to be undertaken, some with significant UK academic library involvement.
- The Teaching and Learning Technology Programme (TLTP), which provided opportunities for experimental projects to explore effective ways of using ICTs in teaching and learning.

- Campus-Wide Information Systems (CWIS), which provided software to deliver general university information across the campus network and were often managed by the library.
- The National Information on Software and Services (NISS) service, particularly its bulletin board which became heavily used very quickly.
- The Combined Higher Education Software Team (CHEST) service, which was set up to negotiate 'deals' with suppliers of IT-related products on behalf of the higher education community as a whole.
- The Oxford Text Archive, a service provided by Oxford University Computing Services which enabled scholars to deposit electronic texts.

There was also considerable informed debate within the profession on the future impacts of IT on libraries. Interesting examples of thinking at this time are provided by the *Information UK 2000* Report (Martyn, Vickers and Feeney, 1990) and the working papers of the Follett Committee's Information Technology Sub-Committee (Higher Education Funding Councils, 1993).

The Electronic Libraries Programme

eLib, the Electronic Libraries Programme, provided UK academic libraries with access to some of the most advanced thinking and practice in the broad area of electronic library service development, and gave a high proportion of academic libraries experience of electronic service development projects. It would be difficult to exaggerate the importance of eLib, without which UK academic libraries might still be struggling to demonstrate their relevance in the rapidly evolving IT-intensive information world.

There were three calls for proposals under eLib, the first two of which yielded a wide range of projects under a number of themes. These were:

- Electronic Publishing
  - Electronic Journals
  - Pre-prints and Grey Literature
  - Quality Assurance and Teaching
- Learning and Teaching
  - On Demand Publishing and Electronic Reserve

- Digitization and Images
- Resource Access
  - Document Delivery
  - Access to Network Resources (the Subject Gateways)
- Training and Awareness
- Supporting Studies.

The emphasis in these phases was on involving a wide cross-section of the higher education library community in relatively small projects. The methodological emphasis was very much on action research, and it was accepted that much of the value would occur through the involvement of professional staff in the research, development and implementation process.

Phase 3 of eLib saw a shift of emphasis, with four main approaches and rather fewer participants in new projects:

- Hybrid Libraries
- Clumps or Large Scale Resource Discovery
- Digital Preservation
- Turning projects from phases 1 & 2 into services.

The concept of the *hybrid library* was discussed in Chapter 3. The relationship between hybrid libraries and *clumps* has been described as follows:

> A complementary idea emerges when the individual library is considered in its broader context. This context may be geographic - for example, within a metropolitan area. It may be based on subject domain, such as medicine or music. It could be created from a commonality of interest - as for example with the major academic libraries in the Consortium of University Research Libraries (CURL). For the individual user there is a need to present these groups as if they were a single resource - they are brought together as a 'clump'. The clump will . . . be presented through a consistent interface - indeed for many purposes the user may not need to be aware that the different libraries even exist. So, for example, the 'music' clump could be presented as a single resource, available to users of all its constituent libraries. For some services, of course, the source library will need to be known - for

example, when the user decides to go and consult the physical stock. The management of the clump is complex, because it relies on cooperative agreements between different libraries which have different resources, different clienteles and different missions.   (Brophy and Fisher, 1998)

A further issue is that of *dynamic clumping*, which occurs when the collection of different libraries or other resources is put together in response to a user's request. To achieve this, *collection descriptions* which are meaningful to software are essential. It was in recognition of this that a Collection Description Focus was set up at UKOLN in June 2001 to provide advice and guidance on, and to encourage the development of, standardized collection description metadata (see www.ukoln.ac.uk/cd-focus/).

The eLib projects can be considered under the following headings:

- The Hybrid Library
- Large Scale Resource Discovery (Clumps)
- Digital Preservation
- Electronic Document Delivery
- Electronic Journals and Pre-Prints
- Subject-Based Gateways
- Other projects

The most significant of these projects are described below.

The Hybrid Library

- AGORA, which demonstrated cross-catalogue 'intelligent' searching together with unmediated document delivery.
- BUILDER (Birmingham University Integrated Library Development and Electronic Resource), which demonstrated the integration of resources at the local library level, including data banks of resources such as examination papers.
- HEADLINE (Hybrid Electronic Access and Delivery in the Library Networked Environment), which contributed to understanding of user authentication issues while building prototype services.

- HyLiFe (Hybrid Library of the Future), which explored management and user-centred issues in the deployment of hybrid libraries, including distributed environments.
- MALIBU (MAnaging the hybrid LIbrary for the Benefit of Users), which produced useful theoretical models of hybrid library services in addition to prototype hybrid library implementations in three institutions.

Large Scale Resource Discovery (Clumps)

- CAIRNS, a clumping of the 25 Scottish academic library catalogues and that of the National Library of Scotland, together with that of one public library authority (East Dunbartonshire). Like other clumps projects, CAIRNS experimented with 'dynamic clumping' based on collection strengths and use of the Conspectus methodology (see Chapter 8).
- M25 Link, based on the M25 consortium (see Chapter 3) in the Greater London area, which provided cross-searching of catalogues based on subject collection descriptions.
- Music Libraries Online, which brought together the catalogues of the major music libraries in the UK. This, rather surprisingly, was the only subject-based clump funded under eLib.
- RIDING, which demonstrated the deployment of a regional clump enabling cross-searching of Yorkshire libraries. Unusually, the consortium included a public library (Leeds) and a national library (the British Library).

Digital Preservation

The most significant project in this area was CEDARS, based on the Consortium of University Research Libraries (CURL), which examined a broad range of issues concerned with preservation of digital information and producing guidelines. It worked closely with the British Library's National Preservation Office (NPO), which is now the focus for work in this area in the academic sector.

Electronic Document Delivery

- SEREN (Sharing of Educational Resources in an Electronic Network), a co-operative development involving the Welsh higher education institutions in developing resource sharing as an alternative to established interlibrary loan, including end-user requesting.
- LAMDA (London and Manchester Document Access), a project similar to SEREN involving resource sharing between a group of London libraries (initially London School of Economics, King's College, University College and the University of Westminster) and a group in Manchester (the CALIM libraries), with article supply priced below the rate charged by the British Library. LAMDA developed into a full service and was the basis for the Docusend project (see below).

Electronic Journals and Pre-Prints

- Electronic Law Journals (ELJ) Environment, which explored organizational and economic factors in moving to electronic journals produced by academics for academics. Working in the field of law, it produced the electronic *Journal of Information, Law and Technology* (JILT).
- NewsAgent, an innovative approach using push technologies to deliver news items to the end-user's desktop on the basis of personal profiles. Its initial implementation was in the field of librarianship but unfortunately it was unable to move from an R&D project to a sustainable service.

Subject-Based Gateways

These are catalogues of internet resources which have been carefully selected and described by experts in the field, so as to provide users with access to quality-assured resources on which they can rely (see Law and Dempsey, 2000). The subject-based gateways funded under eLib have subsequently been replaced by the Resource Discovery Network, described later in this chapter. Among the gateways eLib funded were:

- ADAM (Art, Design, Architecture and Media Information Gateway), led by the Surrey Institute of Art and Design

- Biz/ed (Business Education on the internet), led by the Institute of Learning and Research Technology at the University of Bristol
- EEVL (Edinburgh Engineering Virtual Library), led by Heriot-Watt University in Edinburgh
- OMNI (Organizing Medical Networked Information), led by the University of Nottingham
- SOSIG (Social Science Information Gateway), again led by the Institute of Learning and Research Technology at the University of Bristol.

Other eLib projects

- ROADS (Resource Organisation and Discovery in Subject-based services), which developed a series of software tools for use by other projects, especially the subject-based gateways, including software for:
    - creating, editing and deleting resource descriptions
    - creating browsable listings of resources
    - creating searchable indexes
    - undertaking maintenance tasks such as link checking, so that broken links are repaired automatically
    - translating between description formats.
- HERON (Higher Education Resources ON-demand), which developed a national database and resource bank of electronic texts, together with rights clearance mechanisms. The idea behind this service is that it is far more efficient to clear rights nationally and to maintain a record of which library holds which resources than for each library to try to do this on its own.
- MODELS (Moving to Distributed Environments for Library Services), which has provided the theoretical functional structure for much subsequent development through the elucidation of the influential MODELS Information Architecture (MIA).
- Netskills (Network Skills for the UK Higher Education Community), which has produced a range of highly regarded training materials for internet users in higher education, including a web-based tutorial intended for independent learners. Netskills materials have been made available to institutions for them to exploit and many are used within information skills tuition.

The Distributed National Electronic Resource

In 1999 the JISC, recognizing that to date many developments had not been co-ordinated, sought to develop a framework within which electronic services could be developed and deployed. The framework was initially called the Distributed National Electronic Resource (DNER), described by the JISC in the following terms:

> The Distributed National Electronic Resource (DNER) is a managed environment for accessing quality assured information resources on the Internet which are available from many sources. These resources include scholarly journals, monographs, textbooks, abstracts, manuscripts, maps, music scores, still images, geospatial images and other kinds of vector and numeric data, as well as moving picture and sound collections. (JISC, 1999)

The vision for the DNER argued that there are four major components which are needed to enable electronic resources to be useful in learning, teaching and research. These are:

- The network technology: including the physical networks that link institutions, as well as the internet itself and the world wide web.
- Digital resources: a body of electronic material. In 1999 the JISC argued that 'We are fast approaching the point of critical mass at which people automatically turn to networked digital resources as their first choice when seeking information'. We have almost certainly passed that point now.
- Complementary networks: on its own JANET is not enough. To create a truly national resource there is a need to develop complementary networks (such as the People's Network for public libraries and the National electronic Library for Health), and to do so in a co-ordinated fashion that enables interoperability.
- A learning society: a broad social environment that places learning at the head of its list of priorities.

The components of the DNER could therefore be seen as:

- The communications networks
- The content

- Interfaces, navigation and delivery mechanisms
- System management
- Delivery services. (JISC, 1999)

A new round of development activity was funded, taking its name from the Call document and becoming known the 5/99 Programme. A major driving force behind this Programme was the perceived need to make the electronic services more relevant to learning and teaching, since previously the emphasis had been on serving researchers and those on advanced courses. The 5/99 Programme had two major themes:

1   The implementation and development of the DNER infrastructure itself. Work was funded on:

- subject portals, building on the subject gateways developed in eLib and now funded as part of the Resource Discovery Network (RDN)
- document delivery, including the Docusend project which was built on the experience of Lamda
- underlying systems to enable interoperability, for example through deployment of 'brokers' using Z39.50 or other protocols for the interchange of data between systems.

2   The development of new content and services in support of learning and teaching. Here projects, which were extremely diverse, included:

- Virtual Norfolk
- The Interactive Content Exchange (ICONEX)
- Digital Egypt
- Television and Radio Index for Learning and Teaching (TRILT).

The JISC Information Environment

While the above Programmes were under way, JISC took the strategic decision to redefine the framework for national academic information services, partly because the term DNER had not found widespread acceptance. The new term was the 'JISC Information Environment' (IE), and it would be designed to 'provide a range of services, tools and mechanisms for colleges and universities to exploit fully the value of online resources and services. It will enable presentation, delivery and use of online resources in ways tailored to support individual and institutional requirements in learning, teaching and research' (JISC, 2003). The strategy envisaged four strands of development:

1   'Doorways to the future', concerned with the development of portals which are able to access information across disparate sources and present results seamlessly to the end-user. Part of the challenge is to ensure that each user receives the copy most appropriate to him or her.
2   'Making the most of our wares', designed to provide tools and services to help institutions to create and share resources across networks.
3   'Joining up delivery', which focuses on shared services, i.e. the services (such as user authentication) which electronic services need to be able to access in the background in order to provide the user with the necessary services.
4   'From libraries to learning', which is concerned with joining up electronic library services with virtual learning environments (VLEs).

The architecture of the IE is instructive in demonstrating how the different components fit together (see Figure 5.1).

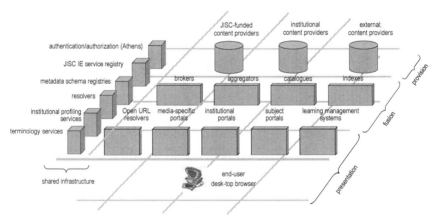

Figure 5.1   The architecture of the JISC Information Environment
(Reproduced by permission)

At the top of the diagram there is a 'provision' row, consisting of different providers of content such as those which JISC itself has funded in its various programmes. In the middle row we have 'fusion' services: these are able to take metadata about content and bring it together in useful ways: the library catalogue is one such service. It holds metadata (catalogue records) about books in a particular library and brings this data together in, for example, subject groupings. The third row, at the bottom of the diagram, consists of systems with which the end user may interact directly. These 'presentation' services make use of the fusion layer and the provision layer to deliver content to the user.

To the left of the diagram there are a number of 'shared' services which are needed to enable the other components to function together efficiently and effectively. These include terminology services, so that another service can look up the preferred form of a subject or other term, resolvers which help determine which copy is most appropriate for a particular user and authentication/authorization services which enable systems to check that the users are who they say they are, and then to check that they have the requisite usage rights. These components, and the overall architecture, are described in some detail in Powell and Lyons (2001) while current developments are documented on the UKOLN website.

Higher and further education data services

JISC and a number of other bodies such as the ESRC now fund the deployment of a wide range of data services for the benefit of students and staff in UK higher and further education. The general modus operandi is that JISC negotiates a 'deal' with the owner of the data and then decides, usually by a competitive process, which of the data centres, or sometimes another specialist agency, should hold it. JISC operates through a Collections Team which is advised by a number of working groups, including an eBooks working group, an images working group and a journals working group.

As we have seen, the normal method of funding dataset deals has been a mix of JISC funding – which in effect is 'top-sliced' from the universities' funding council income – and annual subscription charges paid by institutions which choose to use the service. The major services are described briefly below, while a full list of resources for which negotiated subscriptions are available is available on the JISC website (see www.jisc.ac.uk/index.cfm?name=collbrowse). The datacentres are free to offer additional, non-JISC, services if they so choose and may charge for these on their own terms.

MIMAS

Manchester Information and Associated Services (MIMAS) originally concentrated on non-bibliographic data services but more recently it has broadened the base of services offered and it now offers the widest range of services to the UK academic community. Services include:

- Bibliographic reference services including COPAC (the Online Public Access Catalogue of the Consortium of University Research Libraries), the Archives Hub (which provides links to archival collections in UK universities and colleges), the ISI Web of Knowledge (a massive dataset which includes the various citation indexes) and the zetoc table of contents alerting service.
- Electronic journals, of which perhaps the most important is the JSTOR mirror. JSTOR is an archive of important journals which have been converted into electronic form. This includes many journals of historical importance, including the *Philosophical Transactions of the Royal Society of London*.
- Scientific data, including the Beilstein CrossFire collection of chemical structures data
- Spatial datasets, including satellite and digital map data, for example from Bartholomews.
- Socio-economic datasets, including the UK Census of Population Statistics and various key government survey data, including the General Household Survey, Family Expenditure Survey and the Health Survey for England.

EDINA

EDINA offers a variety of bibliographic, geographic and data services. These are presented in a novel way by offering visitors to the website a series of 'rooms' in which they will find resources of interest. The rooms are:

- The Reading and Reference Room, with a wide range of subject related datasets
- The Map and Data Place, which gives access to Ordnance Survey data.
- The Sound and Picture Studio, which provides still images, films and video
- A Subject View
- A Learning and Skills Centre, which provides access to NLN materials among other resources
- A Digital Conservatory, a new initiative funded by the JISC and the UK eScience Core Programme which will provide services to manage and curate huge datasets, such as those transmitted by observational satellites.

BIDS

Bath Information and Data Services (BIDS) was the first of the JISC datacentres and hosts a range of dataset services. However, it is no longer directly funded by JISC. Its services include:

- the INSPEC data services from the Institute of Electrical Engineers, which provide abstracts of over 4000 journals in the field
- the International Bibliography of the Social Sciences (IBSS)
- ingentaJournals, a full-text document delivery service covering about 2000 journals and offering access to well over a quarter of a million full-text articles. ingenta operates a number of other services, including HERON, which is an example of an eLib project which became established as a service and was then taken over by a commercial organization.

AHDS

The Arts and Humanities Data Service is jointly funded by the JISC and the Arts and Humanities Research Council (AHRC) and provides archival and access services for major datasets in the arts and humanities with specific foci on archaeology, history, literary, linguistic and other textual studies, the visual arts and the performing arts. Although its actual service provision is distributed, it operates through an executive based at King's College London.

AHDS, in addition to securing the long-term preservation of important datasets and making arrangements for their access, has been a leader in the development and promotion of appropriate standards and agreements. These range from the technical standards which must be met by collections deposited with AHDS to standard agreements on rights management.

The UK Data Archive

Based at the University of Essex, the UK Data Archive is funded by the ESRC and JISC and provides storage of and access to a very wide range of predominantly social science data. It is the lead partner in the Economic and Social Data Service (ESDS) which is a joint initiative with MIMAS, providing web access to regularly updated international datasets.

Because much of the material available at the Data Archive is raw data, users can invoke software to perform real-time analyses from their workstations. This is important because a lot of work in the social sciences involves modelling economic and societal trends.

EduServ

A not-for-profit company set up in 1999 by the Universities of Bath, Southampton and East Anglia, with the support of JISC and HEFCE, EduServ is an umbrella organization for a number of services which those universities had hosted for some years, including CHEST, NISS and ATHENS.

CHEST (originally the *Combined Higher Education Software Team*) negotiates contracts for the supply of software and other IT-based products on behalf of higher and further education in the UK. A typical 'deal' will consist of an educational discount price for a piece of software, available to all universities. CHEST has also been responsible for negotiating the deals with data suppliers which have resulted in the services offered through the datacentres, as described above.

ATHENS is an access management or 'authentication' system which aims to provide 'single sign-on' for users throughout UK higher education. In other words, each user should need to have only one user name and password, and the ATHENS system then handles the authentication requirements of each service automatically. This saves the user having to remember multiple user names and passwords, and having to type them in for each service accessed. The ATHENS administrator at each site has facilities to manage that site's accounts, so that, for example, all its users in a particular category could have access privileges to a particular data service changed at the same time. Although ATHENS cannot at present cover all the resources used by academic libraries and has some other limitations, it represents a major step forward for users and for the management of their access. It is administered centrally by EduServ.

The JISC National Mirror Service has recently been transferred to EduServ. The intention behind this service is to provide up to date copies (mirrors) of software and other electronic materials which are of interest to the academic community. The service holds in excess of 1 terabyte (a thousand billion bytes or a thousand gigabytes) of data available for downloading.

The Resource Discovery Network

Set up in 1999 as a means of providing UK higher education with access to quality-assured internet resources, the Resource Discovery Network (RDN) consists of a central co-ordinating body, the Resource Discovery Network Centre (RDNC), and a number of 'hubs', many based on the earlier eLib subject gateways.

Each of the hubs provides a gateway to internet resources whose quality has been checked by experts, and a variety of other subject-related services. These include databases of various kinds, mirrors of resources held elsewhere in the world and archives of discussion fora.

The RDNC, which is run by MIMAS, has responsibility for overall development of the RDN. It undertakes promotional activities, sets standards, provides a high level 'Resource Finder' to enable users to access all the hubs' records in one search and offers support to the hubs as and when this is needed.

The current hubs are:

- Artifact, for the arts and creative industries
- EEVL, for engineering, mathematics and computing
- GEsource, for geography and the environment
- BIOME, for health, medicine and life sciences
- ALTIS, for hospitality, leisure, sport and tourism
- HUMBUL, for humanities
- PSIgate, for physical sciences
- SOSIG, for social science, business and law.

Gateways and portals

Although the term 'gateway' has been in use for some years, attempts have been made in the context of the IE to define more precisely what is meant by this concept, and also to introduce the idea of the 'portal'. Although these terms are sometimes used interchangeably, the IE definitions suggest that a gateway is in essence a tool for pointing users to resources available elsewhere. So, for example, a user will access the gateway to identify a quality-assured web resource, but then by clicking on that resource's URL will switch to the resource itself, leaving the gateway for the time being. A portal on the other hand uses worldwide information resources to build added-value services, so that the user's request may be used to generate a query to a variety of other services, but the results are then interpreted by the portal and delivered to the user. In essence, the user does not leave the portal to get a response. Although there is clearly some overlap, these distinctions are important in understanding the likely development path for the IE.

Working together: the need for ICT standards

It is fairly obvious that if libraries and users are to be able to use the myriad services on offer effectively, there must be some standardization of design and implementation. The IE rightly depicts standards as one of the cornerstones for its development. The key issue is one of *interoperability*: ensuring that all the information systems, the servers and clients (these last being the end-user software systems) can work together meaningfully. This is a huge subject, and is occupying the attention of all the major software and information companies in the world as well as many academic researchers. The world wide web has its own collaborative standards forum (the World Wide Web Consortium (W3C)), dedicated to web standards, but of course there are many other areas where standardization is essential. Perhaps the best guide to appropriate standards in the academic library field is that produced by UKOLN, which provides advice under the following headings (UKOLN, 2004):

- Web standards and file formats
- Distributed searching
- Metadata harvesting
- News and alerting
- Context-sensitive linking
- Transactional services
- Authentication and authorization
- Metadata usage guidelines
- Service registry.

While it is beyond the scope of this book to go into detail on standards, it is worth reiterating that they provide the 'glue' which enables important concepts like the IE to be developed. Applications and services which do not use widely accepted standards should be treated with great suspicion and avoided unless there is overriding evidence in their favour.

Conclusion

There can be no doubt that information and communications technologies have been the biggest influence on academic library development during the last decade. In the UK the sector has willingly grasped the opportunities presented and, through the eLib and other programmes, has made rapid advances in the exploitation of technology. The Follett Report was timed to perfection as far as academic libraries were concerned: it put in place the investment needed to upgrade buildings but also enabled experimentation and development at exactly the time that the enabling technologies were reaching their first maturity. The challenge now is to build on the achievements to date and achieve real integration of information and library services into learning and research environments.

References

Brophy, P. and Fisher, S. (1998) The Hybrid Library, *The New Review of Information and Library Research*, **4**, 3–15.

Higher Education Funding Councils (1993) *Libraries and IT: working papers of the information technology sub-committee of the HEFCs' Libraries Review*, UKOLN.

Joint Information Systems Committee (1999) *Description of the DNER* and *Adding Value to the UK's Learning, Teaching and Research Resources: the Distributed National Electronic Resource (DNER)* www.jisc.ac.uk/index.cfm?name=dner_description
and
www.jisc.ac.uk/index.cfm?name=dner_adding_value

Joint Information Systems Committee (2003) Investing in the Future: developing an online information environment, www.jisc.ac.uk/uploaded_documents/Investing%20in%20the%20Future%20v4.pdf.

Law, D. and Dempsey, L. (2000) A Policy Context – eLib and the emergence of the subject gateways, *Ariadne* 25,
www.ariadne.ac.uk/issue25/subject-gateways/intro.html.

Martyn, J., Vickers, P. and Feeney, M. (1990) *Information UK 2000*, Bowker-Saur.

Powell, A. and Lyons, L. (2001) The DNER Technical Architecture: scoping the information environment,
www.ukoln.ac.uk/distributed-systems/jisc-ie/arch/dner-arch.html.

UKOLN (2004) JISC Information Environment Architecture: Standards framework. Version 1.1,
www.ukoln.ac.uk/distributed-systems/jisc-ie/arch/standards/.

Further reading

JISC Services:

AHDS
www.ahds.ac.uk/
BIDS
www.bids.ac.uk
CHEST
www.eduserv.org.uk/chest/

COPAC
    www.copac.ac.uk/
Data Archive
    www.data-archive.ac.uk/
EDINA
    www.edina.ac.uk/
ingenta
    www.ingenta.com/
MIMAS
    www.mimas.ac.uk/
RDN
    www.rdn.ac.uk/
UKOLN
    www.ukoln.ac.uk/

6
Human resources

Introduction

Staff are responsible for delivering services to users and are probably the library's most important asset. A large university library will employ upwards of 100 staff, each with specialist skills, and the co-ordination and management of all this effort to create a coherent service is a major undertaking. In this chapter we will look at the types of staff, in terms of skills and qualifications, which an academic library needs, typical staff organizational structures and the question of staff development – looking especially at the demands made on staff by the emergence of ICTs. We will touch on a number of personnel management issues, but as this is not primarily a management textbook we will not examine these in any depth.

That staff are facing rapid change, and that change itself is becoming a constant, is almost a truism. At its extreme such change could completely alter the librarian's role. Consider the following quotation, albeit from experience outside the academic sector:

> Five years ago, the library at my laboratory used to occupy several large rooms and employ 30 people. It has been replaced by a digital library that is now ten times bigger – and growing fast. This digital library is staffed by only 12 of the original librarians who are now amongst the best html programmers in the company. This digital library has become an essential part of our lives and the work output has gone up tenfold in 10 years.   (Cochrane, 1999)

That comment, coming as it does from a commercial 'library' organization, serves as a useful reminder to take nothing for granted. It would be entirely inappropriate for academic libraries to adopt what we might call the

Cochrane approach wholesale, but changes of this magnitude in one sector do point up the need for a very careful examination of practice in others.

The traditional staffing structure of academic libraries has been hierarchical. So, typically:

- The University Librarian is the senior manager, with responsibilities both for the strategic direction of the library and for representing the library in the university and wider community. In converged services these responsibilities will include the strategic direction of computing services, and the post might then be called something like 'Director of Information Services and Systems'. In these cases there may be a second-tier manager with responsibility for library services and it is possible that this post may carry the title of 'university librarian'.
- At the next level one or more 'Deputy Librarians' (again, actual job titles differ) have responsibility for the overall operation of the library, usually including specific areas such as planning, finance, buildings, etc.
- Section heads (again with any of a variety of job titles, such as the rather unlovely 'Sub Librarian') have responsibility for an operational section, such as reader services and technical services.
- Unit heads (very often called Senior Assistant Librarians) are in charge of operational units such as interlibrary loans, the issue desk or cataloguing.
- Subject librarians, often without managerial responsibilities, have a role involving liaison with academic departments and providing expertise in particular subject areas. They may have responsibility for stock selection in that area, in collaboration with the relevant academic departments.
- Assistant Librarians, the most junior grade of professionally qualified staff, are deployed throughout the library to provide additional professional support, and share a range of common duties such as enquiry desk work.
- Senior Library Assistants, not formally qualified in librarianship, have supervisory responsibilities, for example in the circulation section, usually gaining the position on the basis of long experience.
- Library Assistants are the front-line troops of the library, responsible for work not requiring a professional qualification, including staffing the issue desk, reshelving and tidying books, acquisitions and cataloguing processes.

- Specialist staff, for example where the library runs a bindery or has significant special collections.
- Increasingly, IT specialists – or at least a Library Systems Manager – who sit outside the formal hierarchy because their responsibilities cross all sectional boundaries.
- Manual staff, including caretakers and cleaners: in many institutions staff at these grades come under a central Estates Department rather than under the direct control of the University Librarian.

A variety of pressures have produced significant changes in this traditional picture, including:

- Increased demand for services leading to severe pressures on staff, leading in turn to redeployment into those areas under most pressure.
- Reductions in staffing levels, caused by financial stringency across the higher education sector, with the 'unit of resource' (amount received per student from the government) being reduced every year.
- Recognition of the need for increased flexibility to address new issues and staff shortages, with the consequent blurring of boundaries between staff, including those between professional and so-called 'non-professional' (better called 'paraprofessional') staff.
- A shift towards team-working, recognizing that an effective team makes use of the variety of skills its members can bring to the table regardless of their position in the hierarchy. Teams are particularly appropriate for developing plans and implementing new services. Working groups, brought together to undertake a specific task, have also proved effective and served to loosen hierarchical structures.
- General trends, to an extent encouraged by good management practice elsewhere, to devolve decision making and responsibility downwards and to flatten previously hierarchical structures.
- Recognition that libraries are services and that they need to re-focus on customer needs ('the customer comes first' ethic) rather than, perhaps, on collection building. It then becomes the responsibility of all staff to be customer, rather than task, focused.
- The impacts of information technology, with its tendency to empower staff at lower levels of a hierarchy.

- Integration of services across departments, partly because of IT, including most notably convergence between libraries and computing services departments. Although convergence between libraries and academic departments has been discussed, there is no evidence of it happening.
- A general trend away from 'deputy' posts, on the basis that all senior staff should have substantive responsibilities of their own, and that all that is necessary is that the organization should have the capacity for deputizing when this becomes necessary. The general flattening of staffing structures has also encouraged the demise of the post of deputy.

These pressures, and some of the changes taking place as a result of them, are considered in greater detail below. The specific issue of convergence, which can have enormous impacts for library staff structures, was discussed in Chapter 3.

The impact of electronic libraries on staff

As part of the eLib programme, the IMPEL project, undertaken at the University of Northumbria at Newcastle, carried out detailed studies of the impact that the development of electronic libraries was having on library staff. The words of one of the assistant librarians interviewed summed up the feelings of uncertainty among many library staff at that time:

> We're at that stage where we really don't know what we should be doing next. It's a sort of paradigm crisis stage. We've come to a situation where our traditional library world can't really deal with the way information is going and we don't really know what the new framework needs to be.
> (Edwards, Day and Walton, 1998)

In the intervening years, staff have become more comfortable with the demands that information technology places on them and are more cognisant of the opportunities for new, and improved, services. However, it is important to recognize that IT continues to develop at a rapid pace and change induced by IT is more or less constant. In addition, there are a wide variety of other drivers which are either forcing academic libraries to change or providing them with opportunities to do so. These include alterations in learning and teaching methods, reorganizations within institutions, continuing pressures on budgets, new legislative requirements (such as SENDA) and, inevitably, staff turnover. The inevitability of change should not mask the fact that it needs to be managed and that staff need space in which to adjust to new challenges.

The management of change is a topic which has received considerable attention in recent decades, for it affects all kinds of enterprise. It is discussed further in Chapter 12.

Links with academic departments

For many years librarians have emphasized the close involvement that library staff need to have in the learning, teaching and research processes if institutions are to be effective in their primary mission. Library staff sit uncomfortably in institutional thinking between academic staff, with primary responsibility for teaching and research, and support staff, who have administrative responsibilities. On the one hand, the fact that students often approach librarians for what is in effect tutorial support tends to demonstrate that their role has a clear, mainstream academic element. On the other, it is hard to argue that a member of staff whose primary role is a back-room one, perhaps in acquisitions, and who rarely meets either academic staff or students, still has an 'academic' role.

The dilemma has been felt most keenly by subject librarians, especially where their duties include tuition of students in information skills (see Chapter 4). In further education, posts of 'tutor librarian' were once common and are still not unknown: if the approach to teaching relies heavily on problem-solving, then identifying, selecting, analysing and synthesizing information from disparate sources are central to the learning experience. The question is how the status of librarians who are closely involved in these processes should reflect this type of work.

There was a trend in the 1960s and 1970s to appoint subject librarians on academic grades, but this is now quite rare. To a large extent this change has occurred because academic staff salaries tend to be higher than administrative ones and thus out of favour with managers in times of financial stringency. Salary costs escalate as individuals progress through long scales with annual increments, without having to satisfy meaningful individual progression criteria. For academic staff, the idea of these scales has been that as their expertise develops, and particularly as their research output grows and their teaching responsibilities expand, they should be appropriately rewarded. But it is very rare for library staff to engage in serious research of the kind that would stand up to scrutiny under the peer review processes their academic colleagues experience – such as the Research Assessment Exercises – or to take responsibilities akin to course leadership. The case for automatic progression through lengthy academic scales is thus weakened unless other grounds can be cited, and there has been little success in trying to establish such grounds for librarians. In many universities 'academic-related' scales have been implemented to try to resolve some of these dilemmas. These may parallel the academic scales but have lower effective maxima; indeed there is a move in universities to adopt a common scale for all staff, with responsibilities reflected by the range of scale points for particular posts.

Staff training and development

The Fielden Report, which was contemporaneous with the Follett Report of 1993, recommended that a minimum of 5% of staff time should be devoted to staff training, although it is doubtful if many academic libraries reached that target (John Fielden Consultancy, 1993). However, and not least because of the rate of change of technology, a well thought out staff development programme is essential for every academic library. The programme will be driven by a number of considerations:

- the induction needed when new staff join the library
- the immediate requirements of the library, for example where a new service or software package is being introduced
- specific job-related needs of particular staff, for example if a supplier is introducing a new system for acquisitions data, perhaps using electronic data interchange
- general requirements of the institution, for example to familiarize all staff with a new strategic plan
- health and safety requirements, especially such things as regular refresher training in fire evacuation procedures

- training related to changing legislative requirements, as with SENDA or new legislation on intellectual property rights
- refresher training, to ensure that staff are equipped to undertake tasks competently
- support for the career aspirations of staff.

It is important that the overall programme is *planned*, and it is good practice for a senior member of staff to have responsibility for this. In some areas, very successful collaborative training programmes have been put in place thus enabling institutions to share the load of appropriate training and staff to compare their experiences with others. The North West Academic Libraries (NoWAL), for example, have developed CLIP, the Certificate in Library and Information Practice (see www.nowal.ac.uk/ training/clip/about_clip. htm).

Staff appraisal

It is now usual for staff in higher education institutions to undergo some form of annual appraisal. At its best, appraisal is a positive, two-way process which provides benefits for both the organization and the appraisee. To be effective it is essential that both appraiser (the person carrying out the appraisal) and appraisee (the person being appraised) spend time preparing for the appraisal interview, which will normally be in two parts. First there will be a review of the past year. This should focus on achievements and should include acknowledgement and praise for what has been achieved. It must also examine difficulties, but with the emphasis being on learning the lessons from mistakes, missed opportunities or maybe simply over-optimism in setting targets, not on recriminations. The second half of the interview should be spent looking to the future, setting targets for the year ahead and considering what support, in the form of staff development or other help, the appraisee will need in order to meet the agreed targets. Following the interview, a written record of targets and actions should be agreed. This can be used by the appraiser to assess the overall staff development and other requirements and priorities of the library's staff, can be referred to by both parties during the year, and of course forms an input to the following year's appraisal process.

Although some appraisal schemes were originally linked to performance-related pay (PRP), this is now rare. Indeed performance-related pay is no longer in favour in most institutions, not least because it can be a divisive influence, especially where staff work together in teams. Singling out one member of a team for reward is potentially if not actually divisive and sends out damaging signals about the precedence of individual effort. Effectively, staff find themselves receiving confused messages – on one hand the PRP process rewards individual effort, while on the other managers are encouraging team working!

Appraisal should never be used as an opportunity for disciplinary action. If a member of staff is performing badly, is disruptive or is taking excessive sick leave, or whatever other problem may arise, this should first of all be addressed by the appropriate line manager and then through appropriate formal channels. These will have been put in place by the university's personnel office, which has the expertise to guide managers in these, thankfully rare, circumstances. The emphasis will always be on trying to find a resolution to the problem which recognizes both the legitimate expectations of the library and the circumstances of the employee. In particular, it is vital to acknowledge the personal demands that staff face, for example through family responsibilities, and to find a mutually acceptable solution.

Conclusion

Without dedicated and expert staff no library could operate. Staff are required both to acquire and organize resources and to design and take part in the interaction with users which is at the core of the library's purpose. However, a variety of influences is causing a rethinking of staff structures, with flattening of previous hierarchies and greater emphasis on teamwork. Because the environment is changing rapidly, most obviously through the implementation of ICT-based systems, staff need to update their knowledge and skills continuously and as a result staff development has taken on a new importance. Techniques such as appraisal can be used in a positive way to enable and encourage staff to be at the forefront of their field.

References

Cochrane, P. (1999) What is the Future of Man, Woman and Machine?, *RSA Journal*, 2/4, 64-9.

Edwards, C., Day, J. M. and Walton, G. (eds) (1998) *Monitoring Organisational and Cultural Change: the impact on people of electronic libraries: the IMPEL2 project*, Joint Information Systems Committee.

John Fielden Consultancy (1993) *Supporting Expansion. A report on human resource management in academic libraries, for the Joint Funding Councils' Libraries Review Group* (Fielden Report), HEFCE.

Further reading

Oldroyd, M. (ed.) (2004) *Developing Academic Library Staff for Future Success*, Facet Publishing.

7

Resource management

Introduction

Libraries are expensive services. The buildings from which they operate – even when services are received remotely – are expensive. Specialist staff must be paid appropriate salaries. Acquiring information is costly. IT equipment and software are expensive, not only to purchase but also to maintain and to replace at regular intervals. As a result of all these requirements, the annual running costs of a university library can, and often does, run into millions of pounds. Professional management skills are needed to control expenditure and ensure that the greatest possible value for money is obtained.

Although in this chapter the term 'resource management' is taken to apply to financial resources, a broader definition is possible and this should be borne in mind. The 'resources' of the academic library include not only its budgets, its staff and its stock but also its 'knowledge'. In the corporate sector there have been considerable strides in taking a broader view of 'resources' and the development of information strategies in higher education is one sign that this understanding is also permeating the academic sector. Another is the interest being shown in knowledge management. However, within this broader understanding the careful and prudent management of financial resources is a major issue and one that must not be neglected by academic library managers.

Generally, funding in academic institutions is divided into revenue and capital. Revenue budgets are intended to cover the ongoing costs of the operation: staff salaries, staff development, consumables, minor equipment, heating and lighting, and so on. Capital funding is reserved for major, one-off purchases such as a new building, a major purchase of PCs or the acquisition of a major collection. Inevitably there is a grey area between the two - for example, the purchase of a single PC might well be a revenue item, while the purchase of 100 would almost certainly be classed as capital. Where exactly the distinction is made depends on local financial regulations and other circumstances.

Setting budgets: capital

Because capital budgets fund one-off purchases they will invariably be negotiated individually. The process may be long drawn out, especially for an item such as a new building (see Chapter 9). The first stage will be to make a case for the concept at university level - for example to gain support for and then acceptance of a case that a new library building is needed. Initial broad estimates of cost will be drawn up and fed into the university's long-term planning. At some stage the request will be prioritized and, as it moves closer towards procurement, a detailed study of precise requirements and costings will be undertaken. On this basis a budget will be set and the responsible manager identified. The agreement to go ahead will result in funding being allocated, possibly on a phased basis. Almost certainly these funds will be earmarked for the agreed project and may not be 'vired' to other purposes (i.e. moved from one budget heading to another).

In recent years there has been a tendency for these processes to be short-circuited, especially through the introduction of competitive processes at national level. So, for example, the outcome of the Follett Report created an opportunity for institutions to bid for funding for new libraries, and the funding councils made it clear that other building projects would - unless the case was exceptional - be given lower priority. In these circumstances a new library suddenly shot to the top of many institutions' building priorities!

For very large capital procurements, including buildings, the university will have specific procedures to be followed and it is possible that the person with ultimate responsibility for drawing up budget estimates will be from another department - in this case, most likely from the Estates Department. It is also possible in these cases that external experts will be engaged to advise the university.

Setting budgets: revenue

Revenue budgets are usually allocated on an annual basis, although some institutions determine indicative budgets and then hold back a proportion until the overall financial position of the university is known. This practice reflects the fact that universities rely heavily on income which is related to student numbers, as calculated in November each year. Yet the financial year runs from 1 August to 31 July. For this reason the indicative allocation may be released on 1 August with confirmation or an adjusted budget in, say, December. Some institutions take even longer to finalize budgets, although good practice should dictate the earliest possible agreement so that the sum available can be managed effectively. Otherwise emergency action to constrain expenditure or to spend an unexpectedly high allocation may be necessary towards the end of the year, and this is rarely in anyone's best interests.

The basis of allocation of budgets by the university varies, but most now operate on a historic basis, i.e. this year's budget is related in some way to last year's. This does not mean that there is simply a repetition of the previous year's position. Factors which affect the budget allocated will include:

- overarching university strategies, such as a decision to reduce administrative staffing costs
- the operation of university policies, such as a decision to move to a more student-centred approach to learning, with greater investment in learning resources
- consideration of the balance between broad headings across the university (for example, is there evidence that the academic staffing is being squeezed more than the support staffing?)
- the operation of benchmarks (see Chapter 13) between universities (for instance, is this university spending significantly less per student on books than the UK average?)
- special factors (perhaps the move to a new building with either additional costs, or perhaps anticipated savings).

It will be a matter for the university librarian to make the best possible case for the library each year, always remembering that as a senior officer of the university, he/she also has an obligation to take a strategic, balanced view of budgetary needs across the institution.

A few universities operate on a devolved budget basis under which revenue budgets are allocated to academic faculties and departments, which then 'buy' services from the service departments. In these cases the librarian will have to negotiate a library budget from each of the budget centres, usually with an agreement on the level of service to be provided. At its extreme this system could theoretically result in a department taking a decision to buy its library services elsewhere; however it is unlikely that a university would allow this to happen since a single decision of this nature could jeopardize the long-term future of the whole service and would, in any case, be virtually impossible to police – would that department's students be excluded from the university library building, for example? Although discussions on these 'purchaser led' approaches was quite common in the 1990s, it is unusual now.

A number of alternative approaches to budget allocation have been tried. For example, zero base budgeting (ZBB) works on the basis that historic allocations should be ignored and the needs of every part of the organization assessed from first principles. Again this was popular at one time, but it has fallen out of favour, partly because of the enormous effort needed to gather an adequate information base on which to apply it and partly because institutions have year-on-year liabilities (for example for buildings maintenance and for staff contracts) that make frequent major shifts problematic. Instead the general approach is to take an overall view of the balance between major expenditure headings and adjust revenue budgets to bring them into line.

Managing budgets

Institutions also differ in the extent to which they devolve responsibility for budgets. In general the library book fund and other, relatively small, revenue budgets are the direct responsibility of the university librarian who is accountable for appropriate, effective and efficient expenditure. More detailed accounts of budgetary management will be found in textbooks on the subject of library acquisitions management, such as that by Chapman (2004) (see especially Chapter 9).

Revenue budgets

The librarian will allocate the available budget to a number of headings, such as one for each academic department's library purchasing. This may be subdivided into budgets for books, for periodicals, and for other items, and practice differs as to the extent to which virement is allowed between headings. It is important to stress that these are *library* budgets, and departments should be able only to advise, not dictate, what should be purchased. However if a devolved budgeting system is used in the university, detailed negotiation may be necessary although even here it is desirable that the budget negotiated should be for providing library services, not for each individual item. In addition to the departmental budget headings, there will be allocations for interlibrary loans, for reference and general works, for bibliographies, and so on.

Various mechanisms have been used to determine the amounts that should be 'allocated' to each department, and some academic libraries use complex formulae for this purpose. The most obvious factors are numbers of students, average costs of books and periodicals (whether in traditional or electronic formats), the rate of obsolescence of the subject (which indicates the desirable replacement rate), whether the department has a significant research track record, and how 'library intensive' the subject is. Quantifying these factors, and then assigning appropriate weights to each, is a complex activity and one likely to generate considerable heat, not least from departments who think they are losing out. In the end, professional judgement, possibly exercised through a library committee if there is one, is the most sure way forward.

The management of these budgets will usually, at the detailed level, be the responsibility of acquisitions section staff and subject librarians. They will need to ensure that orders are placed against each budget which will result in that budget being fully spent by the year end. This means that some over-commitment, to allow for books whose publication is delayed etc., will be essential unless the university is willing to allow credit balances to be carried forward, which is now unusual. Careful monitoring of each budget allocation, commitments and expenditure throughout the year will be necessary. Usually, now, expenditure can be monitored online through the library management system (see Chapter 10).

A particular issue will be the way in which expenditure on 'shared' resources is handled. For example, should a publication like *Chemical*

Abstracts be charged in full to the Chemistry Department heading, or apportioned across a range of departments which make use of it, or paid for entirely as a 'central' expense? Although the last option is administratively convenient, it can lead to a high proportion of the available budget being 'top-sliced' for central expenditure, leaving relatively little for departmental headings – this can become a politically sensitive issue.

A further complication lies in the determination of the most efficient way of acquiring publications which are available in a variety of formats. For example, it may be possible to buy a printed version or to subscribe to online versions, the latter available from different vendors with different terms and conditions attached. Library staff need to determine the *life cycle cost* of such items, i.e. the total cost of providing access for users of each option, taking into account such factors as the long-term value of a bought as opposed to a rented resource, the costs of handling and shelving the physical item, the benefits (which can best be thought of as negative costs) of having online access at the desktop and so on. The availability of national 'deals' for some electronic resources, for example through JISC's data centres, further complicates the issue. Cost recovery from users, perhaps by making a per-item charge for interlibrary loans, will also be part of the equation.

Consortial approaches to gaining reduced prices may sometimes be attractive. This was the thinking behind the eLib LAMDA Project and its derivative, Docusend, (see Chapter 5) which sought to enable its members to achieve document delivery at a cost below that of the standard British Library interlibrary loan form. The JSTOR project has attempted to make savings in the costs of shelving and buildings by enabling libraries to discard long back runs of journal titles (Guthrie, 1997).

Staffing budgets

The operation of staffing budgets is more variable than that of other revenue allocations. Options include:

1   Devolving responsibility to the librarian in the same way as other budgets, for expenditure at his/her discretion. Many universities are reluctant to do this because the long-term commitment implied by the

issue of a staff contract makes the overall staff budget difficult to control if every department acts alone.

2   Devolving responsibility to the librarian, but only to operate within an agreed/approved staff structure. The librarian may then make appointments to any vacancies which occur provided they are within the approved structure and the allocated overall budget, but may not invent new posts without specific approval. Of course the more cynical might regard this as a good way for the university to impose cuts, since providing an agreed structure with a budget which is too small forces the manager (in this case the librarian) to freeze posts etc., without central management having to determine which posts. It also encourages managers to keep the cost of each post as low as possible, since appointing to a high point on a scale in effect leads to cuts in posts elsewhere.

3   Keeping the staffing budget centralized and simply providing an agreed staffing structure specifying the number of posts at each level. In effect the librarian has no staffing budget, except perhaps a small allocation to enable temporary cover to be bought in. This can however create problems for the university, since managers have no real motivation to keep costs down.

Most academic libraries face acute pressures on their staffing budgets, no matter which approach is used. It is therefore very important that they use appropriate techniques to ensure that the staffing budget is fully utilized, i.e. that as much staffing 'resource' as possible is deployed throughout the year. This means taking early action when a resignation is received, planning ahead for retirements and ensuring that no avoidable delays occur in the appointment procedures.

In some universities additional allocations may be made for such items as staff development costs, while in others the librarian must make appropriate provision from within the main allocation.

Capital budgets

In general the control of capital budgets will be handled by the finance office, especially where the expenditure is for a major capital asset such as a new building. There will be clauses in the contract which state when payments are due and it will be the responsibility of the estates department or other building professionals to certify compliance in order to allow payments to be released. For some capital projects, such as the purchase of large numbers of PCs, library staff may have responsibility and this will be discharged in the same way as for revenue budgets, with care to ensure that tendering procedures are properly followed.

Financial regulations

All universities operate under stringent financial regulations, which set out who is responsible for authorizing expenditure and the precise procedures which must be followed by anyone involved in spending the institution's funds. It is important to recognize that *all* funds held by the institution's constituent departments, including the library, are institutional funds for these purposes. So, although there may be a tradition or a formal agreement that the library may 'retain' fines income, for example, in strict terms that income is the university's. This is another way of saying that academic libraries, with a very few specialized exceptions, are not legal entities in their own right and must therefore act in all matters as part of the parent body.

The financial regulations will state which officers of the university are responsible for expenditure. Usually, day to day authority for non-capital expenditure is vested in heads of department, of whom the university librarian or equivalent is one. The regulations will state the extent to which such responsibility can be devolved to others – very often this is defined in terms of the maximum amounts individuals at different levels may authorize. For example, section heads might be able to sign orders up to, say, £1000 but anything above that may need the university librarian's signature. As noted above, very large amounts may need to be authorized by the university finance officer or the vice-chancellor. It is worth noting that the annual renewal of the periodicals supply contract can involve a large enough sum to fall within such regulations.

Because libraries order very large numbers of individual items they are usually permitted to operate under slightly different regulations from those applying across the university in general. For example, the general regulation will be that all orders must be placed on official university order forms. For library book orders, especially where electronic data interchange

(EDI) is used, alternative procedures may be authorized. With electronic transactions becoming more common, this is no longer an unusual requirement for the university finance office.

Although we will not examine the issue in detail in this book, co-operative purchasing (where a number of universities come together to negotiate a beneficial 'deal' from a supplier) may introduce additional regulatory requirements. For example, many universities require all departments to make use of such co-operative agreements wherever they are in place. This stops individuals or departments negotiating their own deals. A further issue may be that universities sometimes have a stated preference to use local suppliers where possible, and where no alternative co-operative agreement is in place.

In order to ensure that the financial regulations are being observed and that the university is receiving the best possible value for money for its expenditure, *audit* procedures are put in place. Universities have three 'tiers' of audit: *internal audit* is undertaken by university-employed staff in the finance office; *external audit* is carried out by an external firm of accountants employed for the purpose; *funding council audit* is a high level procedure which enables the funding councils to send a team of auditors into an institution if it so wishes, although this power is rarely used.

The internal audit team usually works to a schedule which ensures that all departments will be examined over a period of years. It also follows up any questionable practices which come to light – for example if it transpires that a department has been ordering from unauthorized suppliers, the audit team could examine the department's procedures and make recommendations for changes. The external auditors are mainly concerned with auditing the accounts, but they also have powers to examine any aspects of the university's affairs which they believe to need investigation. Where either team of auditors makes a formal recommendation for action, the head of the department concerned will be required to respond within a set time period.

Conclusion

Libraries have always been resource-intensive organizations. In the past they spent their non-staffing budgets on books, journals and other paper-based products. With the need to acquire electronic resources the pressures on budgets have intensified, and selection decisions have become much more difficult - the purchase of access rights might compromise long term ownership, but conversely the purchase of printed versions may, especially with user expectations of electronic delivery so high, deny access. The balance between staffing and other budgets must be maintained, but often the librar ian has little control over the former. Working within a framework of institutional financial regulations, the academic library manager has a complex task to balance all the demands on the limited resources available.

References

Chapman, E. (2004) *Managing Acquisitions in Library and Information Services*, 2nd edn, Facet Publishing.

Guthrie, K. M. (1997) JSTOR: from project to independent organization, *D-Lib Magazine* (July), www.dlib.org/dlib/july97/07guthrie.html/.

Further reading

Graham, T. W. (1998) *Overview: resourcing and budgeting issues.* In Hanson, T. and Day, J. (eds), *Managing the Electronic Library: a practical guide for information professionals*, Bowker-Saur, 185–211.

Roberts, S. A. (1998) *Financial and Cost Management for Libraries and Information Services*, 2nd edn, Bowker-Saur.

8

Collection and access management and the organization of resources

Introduction

Library services are based on collections of information materials ('information objects'), whether or not those collections are owned and maintained by the library itself. Although it is theoretically possible for a library to exist, and serve its users, without any collections of its own, this would be highly unusual for any academic library at the present time. Instead most academic libraries operate their services based on a mix of their own and other organizations' collections. So, a university library will have a collection of mainstream books and journals, may have collections of other media such as videos, slides, etc., and 'special' collections such as historical archives, but will also draw on the book and journal collections of other libraries, like the British Library and its document supply services, to supplement its own stock. Electronic collections could include databanks of online information, held locally by the library, but are more likely to be accessed remotely at another organization. Equally the library's collection will include 'virtual collections' accessed through gateways containing carefully selected pointers to useful web pages. It is important to emphasize that this last category is just as much a 'library collection' as the traditional books on shelves. It requires expert staff input to select and maintain and it requires appropriate delivery mechanisms to enable users to access it. Bear in mind also that electronic collections may increasingly be dynamic; that is, their content changes automatically in response to queries received and other factors.

Collection management, sometimes called *collection development*, lies at the heart of the library's tasks. (The term *collection management* is preferred here since it emphasizes that the task is an ongoing and active one, involving stock replenishment, withdrawal and so on, and not simply the acquisition of new material.) Some would argue that the professionalization of librarianship can be traced to the time when responsibility for selection of stock passed from the academic staff to the librarians, such is its importance. To undertake this task successfully requires a thorough grounding in the subject itself, comprehensive knowledge of its literature and, most important of all, excellent understanding of the needs of users, both current and – most difficult of all – future.

Collection management

In the UK responsibility for collection management most usually rests with subject librarians or their equivalent, working closely with academic staff. Although in the USA it used to be quite common to find Directors of Collection Development (or an equivalent title) this was always rare in the UK. Here a deputy librarian will often have collection management as one of their primary responsibilities – in essence this would be discharged as a policy development and co-ordinating role. There may also be a specific member of staff with responsibility for electronic collections.

In order that collection management can be effective, it is essential that it is informed by knowledge of users' needs. The subject specialist will use a variety of mechanisms to ensure that this is the case. As far as undergraduate texts are concerned, activity may centre on extracting reading lists from teaching staff sufficiently far in advance to enable them to be checked, books ordered where necessary and arrangements made for them to be placed in the most appropriate collection – for example, in the short-loan collection where heavy demand is anticipated. The librarian may also want to consider alternative sources of supply, checking, for example, whether a chapter is available in digitized form and might be delivered electronically.

As we noted in Chapter 4, although subject librarians often complain about the difficulty of extracting reading lists from teaching staff, there is room for greater mutual understanding. While teachers are often unaware of the problems created for librarians by sending copies of reading lists to the library late (or not at all), librarians are all too often ignorant of the reasons for this. These include uncertainty about what a member of staff will be teaching in the new academic year and the inconvenience of the library request arriving in the midst of the peak examination season.

Of course, collection management is not informed solely by reading lists - even for undergraduate texts. Meetings with staff, even and sometimes especially if they are informal, can be invaluable in helping librarians develop their understanding of teaching and research needs. Involvement in course planning committees, course team meetings and staff-student liaison groups can be useful, although there is a real danger that librarians who attempt a comprehensive approach to these will find themselves doing nothing else! Formal meetings are important, however, since they feed into formal institutional approval and quality assurance mechanisms, and also ensure that the librarian is not informed solely by the library enthusiasts among academic staff.

The needs of academic staff - as was noted in Chapter 4 - differ from those of students. A major consideration will be the development of sufficient collection *depth* to meet the needs of staff who are researching in very specific and sometimes abstruse areas while providing sufficient *breadth* to meet needs across the university, including cross-disciplinary needs where staff may want to be informed about thinking in a discipline other than their own. A judgement needs to be made about the appropriateness of purchasing and adding items to stock where they are likely to be of interest to only one person or a very small group, and this will depend to a large extent on the library's mission and its collection development policy in that area. So, in a predominantly teaching institution or one where the subject is not regarded as a strategic priority, it may be appropriate to rely more on electronic sources, on interlibrary loan and on staff visiting other libraries. However, where the library has a national role and is recognized for the strength of its collection in the area in question, it is much more likely that purchases will be made.

A considerable body of research has been undertaken into the measurement of the use of collections, and these techniques can be helpful in pointing to deficiencies and areas where collections may be out of balance. At the simplest level, monitoring reservation queues can provide useful information on pressure points, although it must be remembered that a large proportion of users will not bother to place a reservation if an item is not immediately available. Analysis of loan transaction data can also be helpful, and most library management systems can provide basic statistics which highlight the items in greatest demand. More sophisticated monitoring may involve the use of user surveys or checking items left on reading tables at the end of the day.

Some collections will not, of course, be monitored by looking at usage statistics. For example, archival collections may be developed solely through the expertise of specialist staff who will acquire additional stock highly selectively, in some cases through a worldwide network of agents. In such cases collection management will involve considerable emphasis on conservation and preservation (see below), together with careful attention to access arrangements. Scholars who use such collections will be a valuable source of advice and expertise.

The management of collections includes not only the selection and acquisition of new stock, but also the withdrawal of stock when it is no longer contributing to the utility of the collection. Again, of course, where an academic library serves an archival function withdrawal may be a very rare occurrence, undertaken only after careful checking that the item is being preserved satisfactorily elsewhere. But for many collections, and most notably for student-centred collections, material which is out of date or no longer required for a particular course should be withdrawn. This process is considered in the final section of this chapter.

Cataloguing and metadata

One of the major contributions of librarianship to the emerging information society has been a deep understanding of the issues of *describing* information resources in such a way that any particular item can be retrieved reliably and efficiently. The old library card catalogue was the physical embodiment of a great deal of theory and systematic practice: even finding standard ways to record the name of the author of a book has taken enormous effort. Still more effort has been required to agree ways of describing the subject matter of items. It is arguable that one of the major reasons that we still need libraries is that they can bring order to what is otherwise the chaos of the world wide web, where inadequate description of information objects makes effective discovery of relevant items difficult.

While this is not a textbook on cataloguing and classification, it is worth noting that academic libraries almost invariably follow the Anglo-American Cataloguing Rules, version 2 (AACR2) with updates approved from time to time by the Joint Steering Committee for Revision of AACR. In the UK the most common classification system is Dewey Decimal (DDC) while in the USA the Library of Congress (LC) scheme is predominant.

Metadata is a term used for data which describes an information resource, which in its broadest sense may mean an information item (e.g. book, journal paper, image), a collection or an information user. It is sometimes defined as 'data about data'. A catalogue record is the best-known form of metadata in the library environment, but many other examples from other contexts can be cited. There are a wide variety of formats in use for metadata, ranging from the simple keyword approach, as used by web search engines, through structured but generic systems like *Dublin Core* through to highly structured and specialized systems such as the MARC record or the *Government Information Locator Service* (GILS) system.

Stock selection

The selection of items for stock is a highly specialized responsibility which requires not only good subject knowledge and good knowledge of the literature but an ability to anticipate users' needs and draw academic staff's attention to items of potential value. A proportion of material will be selected on the basis of requests from users, most often from academic staff wishing material to be purchased either for student use or to support their research interests. A danger is that purchasing can be biased towards the interests of those staff who are enthusiastic library users, leaving other areas neglected. One of the librarian's tasks is to ensure that this does not happen and that the overall balance of the collection is maintained.

In selecting stock a number of criteria will be used in addition to the subject matter. Knowledge of different publishers will be important, since the reputation of the publisher is a good indicator of quality. The intellectual level of the work will need to be judged: is it a basic introduction, suitable for advanced study or a research monograph? What is its geographical and social bias? Is the author known in the field or a newcomer? Is the work perhaps a new edition of a book that has been well used in the past? Are reviews of the book available? These and other questions will enable library staff to form a judgement on the suitability and likely value of the work to their users.

Types of material

The stock of academic libraries remains predominantly books and journals - in paper or electronic form - together with material in formats appropriate to specific representations, such as slides, other image formats, audio and video tapes and so on. In addition, libraries stock a range of bibliographic tools designed to enable users to access the broader literature.

Bibliographic resources

At their simplest, bibliographies provide no more than bare bibliographic details (author, title, publisher and so on). However, they may be organized in different ways - for example by publisher, by subject, by date - and they may contain additional information either to assist users to determine relevance or to provide locational information. The most extensive entries will provide an abstract or summary of the item in question, and in many cases this will help users to select the relevant items much more precisely than from simple author/title data. Indeed a good abstract may obviate the need to consult the full item.

In the past considerable shelf space has had to be devoted to bibliographic resources in academic libraries. The annual volumes of *Science Citation Index* or *Chemical Abstracts* would require well in excess of a metre of shelving, and over the years the pressure created on library space could be considerable. With the widespread availability of electronic versions of bibliographic resources, these pressures have lessened. Perhaps the most widely used set of bibliographic resources in UK academic institutions are the various JISC services such as the Institute for Scientific Information (ISI) *Web of Knowledge* databases available through MIMAS (see Chapter 5).

In addition to online services which users can access and interrogate (known as 'pull' services since the user 'pulls' information from the database) there are a growing number of 'push' services which deliver information automatically to each user on the basis of their profile of interests. The British Library zetoc service is a good example of this approach (see zetoc.mimas.ac.uk/).

Books

Although the death of the book has long been prophesied, books remain the bedrock of most academic libraries. While paper-based journals (see below) are threatened by electronic versions and equivalents, experiments with ebooks have so far been disappointing. Collections of ebooks are becoming available - examples would be Ebrary, Early English Books Online and NetLibrary - but as yet the evidence for their usefulness and usage, except in very specific circumstances, is limited.

Far from threatening the existence of the paper-based book, ICTs have in some ways enhanced its importance. The volume of books published each year continued to rise throughout the 1990s and sales of books explaining how to use ICT products, such as popular word-processing packages, have been especially buoyant. To the academic library, the term 'books' may be taken to mean far more than the traditional textbook or research monograph, important as these are. Conference proceedings, encyclopaedias, dictionaries, thesauri, yearbooks, guides to organizations, pamphlets, exhibition catalogues and many other categories of publication will all be important.

Journals

Since journals have, traditionally, provided the main route for researchers to report their findings, it is not surprising that they form a major element of academic libraries' stock - in expenditure terms often in excess of 50%. The scholarly journal has its origins in letters exchanged by scientists, which gradually became more and more widely circulated until the need for formal publication was recognized. Launched in 1665, *Le Journal des Savants* in France and the *Philosophical Transactions of the Royal Society* in the UK are generally recognized as the first scientific journals. There are various ways of categorizing journals, but one important distinction is whether or not papers submitted to the journal undergo a *peer reviewing* process as described in Chapter 1.

For all their dominance of scholarly communication it has long been recognized that printed journals have their disadvantages and deficiencies. For example:

- The elapsed time from submission of a paper to publication is frequently in excess of 12 months, which is a serious problem in any rapidly changing discipline.
- Subscription costs of key journals are high, partly because they are in effect a monopoly since, by definition, publication in related journals is less prestigious.
- The costs of distribution and handling are high (for example, the staffing costs involved in claiming and supplying missing issues).
- Storage costs are high since long back runs need to be shelved even if they are little used.

In recent years there has been an upsurge in interest in *electronic journals* and *eprints* which are seen as addressing many of the above problems. In the UK academic sector a number of experiments have been undertaken and reliable, sustainable electronic journal and eprint services are now starting to emerge. Among the experiments and proto-services were:

- the University of Aston's use of the ADONIS biomedical service, described in Chapter 5
- research studies at Loughborough University, including the BLEND and QUARTET projects
- other eLib and JISC-funded work, such as Electronic Law Journals (ELJ) and the Internet Library of Early Journals (ILEJ)
- the Pilot Site Licence Initiative (PSLI), established in 1995 to offer printed *and* electronic versions of journals from Academic Press, Blackwell Press, Blackwell Science and the Institute of Physics.

Among current services available to UK academic users are:

- the National Electronic Site Licence Initiative (NESLI), operated by MIMAS; NESLI (the current version is NESLI2) has replaced the PLSI
- ingentaJournals (formerly JournalsOnline and developed as part of the BIDS datacentre at Bath University), now part of a commercial

company, which provides access to a growing number of major publishers' journals (e.g. those of Academic Press, Blackwell Science, Elsevier Science, John Wiley, Oxford University Press). Papers are provided in HTML or PDF format

- OCLC's FirstSearch, which provides access to full text from over 6000 periodicals, more than 85 databases, and almost 2100 full-image journals and enables the local library to link in its own holdings data.
- Emerald, which specializes in management, including library and information management, journals.

In general, the electronic journals available to date have mainly been 'surrogates' of paper-based journals and even those which have been published in electronic-only format have followed traditional publication processes. However, this is likely to change and experiments with interactive online journals and with multimedia content will undoubtedly lead to new forms of electronic journal.

Eprints

The term eprint is not always used consistently, but it includes:

- Preprints, which are released by authors in advance of peer review both to inform colleagues about important findings and to invite comments
- Postprints, which are equivalent to the peer reviewed paper accepted for publication in a journal

In recent years there has been a growing movement to persuade academic authors to self-archive their publications so that copies can be made freely available to the academic community without libraries having to pay huge subscription costs. Part of the argument behind this movement is that universities already pay the full cost of undertaking research, so why should they then give the results away to commercial publishers and then, to add insult to injury, have to pay to access it? In 2003 the Berlin Declaration was approved by a gathering of influential experts (Max Planck Society, 2003) and has provided the basis for persuading universities to become signatories to the movement. The influential Budapest Open Access Initiative (BOAI) provides support for this activity in Europe, while the Open Archives Initiative (OAI) is providing technical and other support worldwide.

In the UK, the JISC has been very active in this field and in 2003 launched a research and development programme called Focus on Access to Institutional Resources (FAIR). Projects in this programme are exploring not only the development of institutional archives for research publications, but are also examining electronic thesis collections and the integration of learning object collections with other information resources. The SHERPA project (www.sherpa.ac.uk/), which is part-funded by CURL, is providing a focus to assist institutions to set up their own repositories.

Collection evaluation

A number of methods are available to evaluate collections, including statistical techniques based on usage and issue counts. In general there are two possible approaches: collection-centred and user-centred. The former lays stress on the collection itself and usually involves checking a particular collection against some kind of standard list, which is intended to reveal how 'comprehensive' the collection is. The *Conspectus* methodology, developed by the Research Libraries Group (RLG) in the USA, is the dominant example of this descriptive approach. Codes are given to each subject collection to indicate the collection's strength, linguistic and geographical coverage and intellectual level. In the USA the RLG and the Association of Research Libraries (ARL) together developed the North American Collection Inventory Project (NCIP) to provide an online database of collection strengths. Similar work in the UK has been undertaken under the aegis of CURL.

More recently, greater emphasis has been given to user-centred collection evaluation. The techniques used vary, but may include user satisfaction surveys or simply examination of usage statistics. Gorman and Miller (2001) argue that 'methods are needed that are less labour-intensive, methods that focus on recognizing and meeting user needs more than admiring or critiquing the completeness of collection'. These approaches will need to be integrated into the library's overall performance assessment, a topic discussed in Chapter 12.

Preservation and conservation

It has long been recognized that one of the major threats to libraries arises from the deterioration over time, either gradually or suddenly, of the materials which they hold. Paper deteriorates, especially if the publisher has not taken care to select a paper which has suitable qualities for long-term survival. Poor quality paper is not simply a modern phenomenon: mass production of paper from the mid-19th century onwards has led to a series of problems, including the action of acids left over from the manufacturing process which break down the cellulose which gives paper its structure and strength. Other problems include the use of unsuitable bindings, of which so-called 'perfect binding' in which the edges are simply glued is one of the best (or, rather, worst) examples; the increase in air pollution especially in major cities; the use of unsuitable heating and air conditioning systems; and simply, frequency of use. Use of books results in wear, in the introduction of acids and grease from over-handling, and in deterioration caused by processes such as photocopying. Libraries themselves can contribute to deterioration, for example through inappropriate or overcrowded shelving.

Added to these problems are the possibilities of catastrophic loss caused by events such as fire or flood. The interactions here can be complex – it is not unknown for the water used to douse a fire to cause more damage to the bookstock than the fire itself. The now almost universal preference for metal shelving with open backs aids the spread of fires, partly because the openness of the shelving allows the fire to spread and partly because metal conducts heat much more quickly than does wood. Greater use of electrical equipment increases the risk of fire – as the disastrous fire which destroyed Norwich City Library testifies.

Preservation, conservation and restoration are specialist fields in their own right and detailed treatment is beyond the scope of this book – useful sources of further information will be found in the list of further reading at the end of this chapter. However, policies which encourage good practice in these areas must be the concern of every academic librarian and ultimately every academic library user. These should include:

1   The development of preservation, conservation and restoration policies by the library: these should include priorities (and will of course refer specifically to special collections) and will also define those materials – such as, perhaps, paperback editions of textbooks – which will not be

subject to long-term preservation. The option of digitizing paper-based resources as a means of preservation of content should be considered carefully, although usually originals will need to be conserved also.

2   Basic training for all library staff in the handling (including shelving) of books.

3   Careful consideration of library procedures, including such services as book return boxes (in which books can be damaged if they are dropped a long way or have other volumes dropped on them).

4   The atmospheric control of the library environment. Not every library can afford to have full climate control facilities, but library staff should be aware of the damage that can be caused by repeated *changes* in temperature and humidity. Turning off the heating overnight can be a false economy.

5   The preparation and maintenance of a disaster recovery plan (see Alire, 2000). This should specify the procedures to be followed in the event of a disaster such as a fire or flood. It must specify *who* is responsible for *what*, especially the decision-making responsibilities; where help can be obtained (including the addresses of contractors able to offer bulk freeze drying facilities); how recovery operations should be organized; full plans, descriptions and lists of the building, electrical and other services layouts (so, for example, that a leaking pipe can be identified) and so on. The disaster recovery plan will normally have four sections: prevention, response, reaction and recovery. It is most important that copies are kept to hand *outside the building* by staff responsible for initiating action in the case of a disaster.

A particular area, not covered by the above discussion, but likely to be of increasing concern, is the preservation of electronic materials. There are a number of issues for the academic librarian here:

1   While many electronic resources are purchased on a subscription basis and are not physically held in the library, is the supplier taking steps to preserve the content? If not, is anyone else assuming this responsibility?

2   Where a resource is dynamic (i.e. being updated all the time) what should be preserved? What is being preserved?

3   Where the library does own a copy of an electronic resource, such as a CD-ROM, is it adequately protected for continued use? For long-term use?

4   Where the library, perhaps in conjunction with an academic department, produces an electronic resource, have proper steps been taken to preserve it in the long term? Are back-up copies made, and held in a separate, secure location?

5   Do the media used to hold electronic resources have adequate shelf-life? For example the shelf-life of CD-ROMs is at present uncertain. In ten or 20 or more years' time, will the equipment needed to read the resource still be available? (As an example, consider how difficult it now is to find a PC with a 5¼ in. floppy disk drive.)

The problems of conservation and preservation of electronic media are being considered in a number of initiatives led by the British Library's National Preservation Office, which has a useful website on these matters (see Further Reading at the end of this chapter).

Weeding and relegation

In any collection there will build up over time a proportion of stock which is little used and unlikely to be used in the future. Of course, research collections and those with a long-term preservation function, such as the CURL libraries in the UK, will have retention policies which ensure that material is not discarded simply because it is little used. However, libraries with a mission that emphasizes access to current literature will want to remove such little-used material at regular intervals.

Some material must be removed because it is misleading – old editions of law textbooks would be a prime example, since their advice would be, quite simply, wrong. But with most material a judgement must be made. Statistical data, such as the number of times the book has been issued in the last three years, may be helpful in identifying *candidates* for withdrawal, but it is important that expert judgement is exercised in determining what should actually be withdrawn. Any more general collection evaluation exercises will inform these decisions.

Some academic libraries operate secondary stores where little-used material can be held and retrieved when required – such stores may be on the library premises or at a remote location, and there are some examples of co-operative storage arrangements. In these cases withdrawn material may be held in the intermediate store and usage from the store may provide further indications of continuing value. However, it will still be necessary to withdraw material from the store at intervals and dispose of it.

Disposal may take several forms. Clearly the first consideration must be whether the items have intrinsic value and, where this is suspected, expert advice should be sought. At one time many items were offered to third world countries, but this practice has now diminished and items are now usually only supplied against specific requests. For items not disposed of in this way, it is usual to offer them for sale to members of the university (the out-of-date material that academic staff will buy is a never-ending source of amazement) and, where this fails, to have them pulped.

Conclusion

The management of the library's collections lies at the core of the academic librarian's work. Careful selection of resources – whether they are traditional books and journals or electronic data services – is essential if the library's users are to have access to the information they need. Close liaison with users, and particularly with teaching and research staff, will be essential as will the monitoring of stock usage. The provision of adequate descriptions of resources or metadata is an important function, for without good and consistent resource description retrieval becomes impossible. Much of the collection will need to be conserved for future use, and care will be needed to ensure that it, and indeed the library as a whole, is protected from catastrophic damage. Finally, the librarian will need to review and weed the collections to ensure their continued relevance and utility.

References

Alire, C. (ed.) (2000) *Library Disaster Planning and Recovery Handbook*, Neal-Schuman.

Gorman, G. E. and Miller, R. H. (2001) Changing Collections, Changing Evaluation. In *Collection Management. International Yearbook of Library and Information Management 2000/2001*, Library Association Publishing, 309–38.

Max Planck Society (2003) *Berlin Declaration on Open Access to Knowledge in the Sciences and Humanities*,
www.zim.mpg.de/openaccess-berlin/berlindeclaration.html.

Further reading

Early English Books Online
http://eebo.chadwyck.com/home
Ebrary
http://shop.ebrary.com/
Emerald
www.emeraldinsight.com/
Harvey, R. (1993) *Preservation in Libraries: principles, strategies and practices for librarians*, Bowker-Saur.
JISC FAIR Programme
www.jisc.ac.uk/index.cfm?name=programme_fair
Lee, S. D. and Boyle, F. (2004) *Building an Electronic Resource Collection: a practical guide*, 2nd edn, Facet Publishing.
National Preservation Office
www.bl.uk/services/npo/npo.html
NetLibrary
www.netlibrary.com/Gateway.aspx
Open Archives Initiative
www.openarchives.org/
OCLC FirstSearch
www.oclc.org/firstsearch/

9
The academic library building

Introduction

While the virtual library may or may not be just over the horizon, at present all academic institutions operate their library services from dedicated buildings, and it is highly unlikely that this position will change drastically in the near future. Libraries - in this chapter that term is used of the physical building - form the centrepiece of many campuses and colleges, and frequently their architecture makes a statement about the university itself.

The design of academic libraries is a highly specialized field and one which has benefited from many years' experience by both architects and librarians. To design a new library is a major undertaking for both, and will involve consultation with all the major stakeholders, examination of recent libraries built elsewhere and attention to the smallest detail, coupled with design flair to produce a building which may last for well over a century.

Securing the capital funding for a new library, or funding for major refurbishment of an existing building, is a major task requiring highly developed managerial and political skills. Although in the past making the case was assisted by the existence of 'library space norms' (i.e. standards agreed by government in terms of space per full-time equivalent student) this is no longer the case, and each project must be secured on its own merits. Universities have major building programmes for the extension and refurbishment of their building stock, and the first step is to secure a place in this future programme. This is then followed by lengthy negotiations to secure funding council agreement and an appropriate budget. While the Librarian will be heavily involved in such discussions, they will usually be led by the Director of Finance and the Director of Estates, or their equivalents. Undoubtedly the university Vice-Chancellor will take a keen interest in such a project.

Once agreement to go ahead has been reached, an architect will be appointed (this may be an internal university architect or an external practice) and a detailed programme will be devised. The appointment of the architect is of course a crucial step, and care will be needed to secure the services of someone who has the necessary experience. Visiting examples of libraries designed by different architectural practices will be essential, and it will be important to look not just at the success of the designs *per se* but to ask staff and users about their functionality.

It is usual to set up a committee or steering group to advise the architect and to examine all aspects of the proposed design – obviously it is essential that the Librarian is a member of this group. Clear objectives need to be set and agreement reached on the university's priorities. For example, Revill (1995) reported that the team charged with responsibility for Liverpool John Moores University's Aldham Robarts Learning Resource Centre, to be built on a city-centre site, were set the following objectives:

1. to allow the full potential of the campus to be realised by providing a distinguished and exciting building forming a gateway for the campus from, and to, Rodney Street
2. to create through information technology and planning a highly sophisticated and efficient building for the delivery of learning service
3. to be economical in staffing
4. to be flexible in the use of space
5. to act as a symbolic gateway to the world of learning and the 21st century.

It is interesting to note how such objectives bring together strategic and visionary thinking with practical and workable realities.

Approaches to library design

While the achievement of excellent architectural statements is of great importance, for the library should portray its and its institution's values through its design, the most fundamental issue is that libraries are functional buildings: to adapt Ranganathan, 'Libraries are for use'. It follows that the primary issue for library design is the establishment of expected use patterns and the translation of these into both the general layout and the finest details. Questions which need to be asked at the outset include:

- Which user groups will use the building and what will their pattern of use be?
- What will those users wish to do in the building and what is the balance between different activities?
- How much space, and what kind of space, will be needed to store the library's stock in conditions which will both facilitate expected use and permit long-term preservation for the benefit of future users?
- What services will be offered to users within the building, and what implications do these have both for the use of available space and for the layout of the building?
- What spaces will be needed for library staff to enable them to provide these services?

It is particularly useful to consider some examples of a typical user's interactions with the building when planning the design. For example, one particular user might:

- Arrive at the campus by public transport
  - Where is this in relation to the planned building and its entrance?
  - Will the route be well lit at night?
  - Is the route to the library accessible to disabled people?
- Enter the building
  - Will the entrance be controlled so that users will have to prove their membership before being allowed entry? If so, how will new users be admitted?
  - How will users know where to go next when they enter? For example, which services should be immediately visible?
- Return some books
  - Where will the return point be in relation to the entrance?
- Consult the catalogue
  - How many OPACs will be needed and where should they be sited for maximum convenience and usability?
- Look for books on the shelves

- How will the main sequences be laid out - e.g. in a Dewey sequence by floor?
  - Which collections are likely to be most heavily used? What does this imply for their location?
- Consult the electronic reserve
  - How will electronic services be accessed?
  - How will print facilities be provided?
- Go to the toilet
  - Where should these be situated? How many? What about disabled facilities?
- Look for some refreshments
  - Should there be a coffee bar in the building or will alternatives be available elsewhere throughout the library's opening hours?
- Leave the building
  - How will exits be controlled, e.g. by staff or purely by an electronic security system?

In addition to thinking through such 'walkthroughs' consideration needs to be given to the management and administration of the building and especially to the efficiency with which it can be run. For example, providing an enquiry point alongside each subject collection is desirable but is it affordable?

General principles of design

A number of general principles should inform design. These are:

- *Accessibility*: both in the sense of centrality of position to meet the needs of all users, and in the sense of being physically accessible, especially to people with disabilities. It should be noted that, as discussed in Chapter 11, institutions are now under a legal duty to ensure accessibility to all.
- *Flexibility*: it is impossible to predict future trends, so all areas should be flexible enough to be re-used for different purposes. One of the more common problems occurs when a building has uneven maximum floor loadings so that shelving cannot be placed in some areas.

- *Compactness*: it is desirable that the library's key and most used services should be placed as near as possible to each other, to avoid users having to move around the building too much from one service point to another.
- *Serviceability*: while electrical power and computer network wiring will of course be installed, it should be a straightforward job to replace them, insert new outlets, etc.
- *Environment*: the needs of the library stock for a stable environment should be considered – note also the comments on this issue in Chapter 8.
- *Health and safety*: libraries are used by very large numbers of people and their safety must be of paramount concern.
- *Use of natural light*: reader spaces should be sited to make the most of natural light. The needs of staff who work in the building should also be considered – it is unacceptable to force people to spend their working hours away from all natural light.
- *Comfort*: bearing in mind that users and staff will spend long periods of time in the building, it should be a comfortable place in which to work with due attention paid to all aspects of ergonomics.
- *Maintainability*: the building should be easy and economic to maintain in the long term – at least one university library has been built in the UK with external windows which cannot be accessed for cleaning!
- *Security*: library materials and equipment are vulnerable to theft, so a single entrance/exit with an electronic theft detection system and adjacent staff is essential. Consideration should be given to ensuring good sight lines from staff locations.

A useful source of information on current and recent academic library buildings in the UK is provided by SCONUL on its web site (www.sconul.ac.uk/lib_build/) and includes details of the winners of the annual SCONUL Library Design Awards. Internationally, much useful information on current thinking can be found on IFLA's Library Building and Equipment website (www.ifla.org/VII/s20/slbe.htm).

Information technology

Although this chapter concentrates on the *library* building, in fact most new libraries are being designed as multifunctional spaces with considerable emphasis on the delivery of IT-based services – whether or not the service itself is converged. Many of the issues this raises are dealt with in other sections of this chapter, but it is worth emphasizing the points which need to be considered:

- The building itself must be wired for sufficient power and data both to achieve current planned deployment of IT and in a manner which is flexible enough to permit future, currently unpredicted, needs to be met.
- These needs may include a requirement to provide network connections for users' laptops rather than physical workstations, and this should be considered – usually this will be met by providing a wireless hub.
- Support will be needed at a variety of levels, but there will be much more emphasis on low-level support (e.g. fixing a non-functioning mouse, showing users how to log in) than libraries have traditionally offered.
- Noise from banks of PCs is considerable, and there is more of a culture of noisy study among PC users.
- Heat dissipation can be a major problem in areas where large numbers of PCs are housed, and provision must be made for this when designing ventilation and air conditioning systems.

Noise

Although traditionally libraries have preferred to operate as silent environments, the demands of modern services and of modern teaching and learning methods, to say nothing of user preferences, have changed perceptions. To give two examples: as we have seen above, modern technology, represented by banks of PCs with noisy keyboards, is not particularly conducive to silent working, while group study positively encourages students to talk and discuss their work. In addition, there has been a marked shift in users' attitudes and many prefer to work in more noisy environments than used to be the case.

As a result, the modern library is usually designed with a choice of study and service environments. Reading rooms are commonly split into 'silent',

'quiet' and 'noisy' areas (though the last may not be officially acknowledged) and group study rooms are provided. It is of vital importance that
the design of the building enables such areas to operate successfully. There
must be a clear physical barrier - preferably a wall but failing that banks of
shelving - between silent and quiet areas, otherwise noise will drift across
and the silent area will almost certainly be colonized by noisier readers. It
is also helpful if some library staff are based adjacent to each area so that
they can ask users to observe the rules on noise. Indeed, having a quiet area
to which users can move is one of the keys to successful operation of
'silence' rules.

A further consideration is the siting of services in relation to reading
areas. For example, it is unhelpful to site enquiry points in silent areas since
they will inevitably generate conversation. Even more importantly, facilities
such as photocopiers need to be sited in areas where noise will not be a
problem.

Finally under this heading it is worth considering the effects of the
building's heating and air conditioning plant on noise levels. Curiously, silent
operation is not always essential, and indeed a quiet background noise,
provided it is unvarying, can be helpful in masking extraneous noise - there
have even been suggestions that libraries should install 'white noise'
generators to provide such background. The thinking behind such ideas is
that sudden noises - for example a dropped book - are far less disturbing in
these circumstances than in total silence, while the human ear rapidly
becomes used to the background and edits it out. However, the dividing line
between an acceptable masking noise and an irritating intrusion is a difficult
one to draw and depends as much as anything on individual preferences.
Specialist engineers are able to advise architects on these issues.

Designing reading areas

It is important that libraries provide a variety of study areas suited to
different user requirements. For example, some spaces will be
straightforward reading desks which may need individual reading lights and
it is of course important that a suitable surface is provided (linoleum is
often recommended because it is hard-wearing but has some flexibility as a
writing surface). Other spaces will be equipped with a PC and these will
not normally require individual lighting, but the ambient lighting will be

extremely important to prevent glare on the screen. In addition each work area will require space for books and for making notes as well as for the keyboard and mouse mat.

Attention to detail is very important when designing work spaces. For example, if PCs are provided, have some of them been set up with the mouse placed for left-handed users, some for right-handed? Are chairs suitable for workstation use, but also for writing and reading? Is there somewhere for users to hang jackets and coats - the chair back is perfectly acceptable provided it is designed to take this usage.

Signs and guides

Clear signage is of the utmost importance, not only to enable users to find their way round the building easily but to reduce demands on staff. Indeed it is worth keeping a record of casual queries from users to staff, of the 'where is the . . . ?' variety, as a way of checking on the functioning of library signs.

There is no consensus on the exact nature and layout of library signs, but some of the issues are:

- A consistent signing system should be used throughout.
- Signs should be sited at a height which is in the eye-line of someone standing, which usually means suspended from the ceiling or fixed to a wall at that height.
- Upper and lower case rather than purely upper case should be used as it gives greater visual cues from a distance.
- There should be good colour contrast, with care taken to attend to the needs of people who are colour blind or otherwise visually impaired.
- The number of signs should be kept to a minimum.

With new build it is usual to contract a specialist firm to provide the signage, but attention needs to be paid to the ease and economy with which signs can be moved and replaced. A useful exercise is to ask a few new users to find specific services or areas, and to report back on any difficulties they experience in identifying them. This helps avoid the common fault of a set of directional signs which guide users most of the way and then suddenly stop, leaving the user stranded.

Specialized buildings

In this chapter the emphasis has been on the general-purpose academic library, with the assumption that a range of users, from undergraduates to academic staff, will require its services and its accommodation. From time to time universities have the opportunity to erect a more specialized library, of which one of the best modern examples is the Ruskin Library at Lancaster University. In such a case, entirely different design principles will apply. The Ruskin Library was designed as a 'treasury' for the Ruskin Collection, a priceless and unique collection of the papers of John Ruskin and of items relating to his work and life. The architects described the design philosophy in the following way:

> The linear arrangement is deliberately church-like with entrance, treasury and reading room standing for narthex, choir and sanctuary. The public have access from a double height entrance to the first floor gallery which is arranged as two spaces connected through the treasury by a glass bridge . . . Lighting will be kept to a minimum to preserve the archive . . . the only sunlight allowed into the building will be at sunset which will illuminate the metal soffit running through the centre of the building.   (MacCormac Jamieson Prichard, 1995)

Interestingly, the design of the Ruskin Library and its siting in front of the main University Library greatly influenced the design of the extension to the latter which was 'designed to form a back-drop to the horizontal strata of the Ruskin Library' (ibid., 74).

Conclusion

Buildings remain central to library services and are likely to do so for the foreseeable future, even where many users receive their services remotely. Careful attention to the design of the building and physical service points may make the difference between a well-used and a neglected service. The use of ICTs to deliver services has had major implications for design, and librarians will need to stay alert to its changing influences. Occasionally, the opportunity may present itself for the construction of a building which can serve as a monument to learning, as in the case of Lancaster University's Ruskin Library, and in these cases entirely different design considerations will apply.

References

MacCormac Jamieson Prichard (1995) Lancaster University Library Extension and the Ruskin Library. In Taylor, S. (ed.), *Building Libraries for the Information Age*, Institute of Advanced Architectural Studies, 73-5.

Revill, D. (1995) Liverpool John Moores University: the Aldham Robarts Learning Resource Centre. In Taylor, S. (ed.), *Building Libraries for the Information Age*, Institute of Advanced Architectural Studies, 53-8.

Further reading

Bisbruick, M.-F. and Chaveinc, M. (eds) (1999) *Intelligent Library Buildings: proceedings of the 10th seminar of the IFLA Section on Library Buildings and Equipment, The Hague, August 1997*, K. G. Saur.

International Federation of Library Associations and Institutions, Library Buildings and Equipment Section, www.ifla.org/VII/s20/slbe.htm.

Society of College, National and University Libraries, *Library Buildings*, www.sconul.ac.uk/lib_build/.

Taylor, S. (ed.) (1995) *Building Libraries for the Information Age*, Institute of Advanced Architectural Studies.

10
Library systems

Introduction

All university and further education libraries and virtually all other UK academic libraries depend on IT systems for their basic operations: acquisitions, cataloguing, circulation control and so on. These were originally termed 'housekeeping' systems and although that term is no longer used it serves to emphasize that the purpose of these systems is administrative. A more common current terminology is 'library management system' or LMS. Originally, libraries implemented separate systems for each function and legacies of this situation are still not uncommon – for example many academic libraries still run a separate interlibrary loans system.

The development of IT-based systems by organizations with which libraries deal (such as book and journal suppliers) and within the institution itself (such as student record systems) has meant that much closer attention has to be paid to the integration of the library's systems with others. This requirement is becoming even more of an imperative as heavy use is made of the Internet and world wide web by library staff, suppliers and users and, most especially, as more and more of the information resources to which the library gives access are not held by or owned by the library. Integrating access to the stock of the library with access to remote information sources, and handling the resultant requirements to authenticate and authorize users, are key challenges for the modern academic librarian. Success is dependent on ensuring the *interoperability* of all systems.

The development of academic library systems

At present all UK university libraries use systems purchased from commercial systems suppliers. Although in the early days of library automation it was common for systems to be designed and developed in-house – and some of these systems were remarkably successful – the complexity of modern systems makes this solution inappropriate. Apart from any consideration of development costs, it is impossible to resource maintenance adequately without a large base of system users.

The early development of library systems in the UK was helped enormously by two co-operative research and development projects which received funding from the then Office for Scientific and Technical Information (OSTI), a body most of whose functions have, via various different incarnations, come to rest with the Museums, Libraries and Archives Council (MLA). The Birmingham Libraries Cooperative Mechanisation Project (BLCMP) concentrated on the co-operative development of library catalogues and involved the major academic libraries in the Birmingham area. It is now a commercial company, Talis, and its latest product, called Talis Alto, is one of the leading library systems in the UK academic market. The second project, the South-West Academic Libraries Cooperative Automation Project (SWALCAP), likewise developed a popular system, Libertas, the company becoming SLS before being taken over in 1997 by Innovative Interfaces of the USA. Together these projects and the systems which were developed from them gave UK academic libraries an early lead in this area.

Today there are a considerable number of companies active in this area. In addition to Talis and Innovative, companies with a significant presence in the UK academic library market include Geac, Dynix, Ex Libris, Endeavour and SIRSI. Smaller systems, such as Fretwell-Downing's OLIB and Inheritance Systems' Heritage can be found in specialist academic libraries and in the further education sector.

The LMS is of course only one of the systems which the library has to operate. All academic libraries maintain a website within which their various services can be offered, and this will include the LMS OPAC, access to electronic journals, ebooks and remote databases, resource finders, local databases – for example of past examination papers – general information about the library, lists of selected websites, an enquiry/complaints system, and so on. Recent developments are leading to the redesign of these access points as 'portals', as described in Chapter 5. For library staff, access to the LMS functions may be via a Windows client, since web browsers do not readily provide the functionality, speed of response and security needed for complex transactions which require rapid response times.

Academic library management systems

Although each system differs significantly in the way in which it has been implemented, at the level of basic functions all share common features. In essence the systems are focused on the administration of the library's collections, and the library catalogue – in effect the inventory of the library's stock – has usually formed the core of the LMS. Catalogue records perform a number of functions, encompassing both bibliographic identific-ation and the provision of a definitive record of the library's holdings, the latter including, for example, the number of copies, the site library where each copy is held and associated circulation data to control lending, returns, reservations, etc.

LMS are usually modular, although since most 'third generation' systems now use a relational database model they are in fact highly integrated. However, it is convenient to think of them as offering a series of functional modules including:

- cataloguing
- ordering and acquisition of books and other materials
- serials, including journals, management
- OPAC
- circulation control
- interlibrary loans
- management information.

Many systems will also offer some kind of 'general information' module, sometimes called 'community information' from the parallel public library requirement, although these are becoming less useful with the development of sophisticated websites.

All modern LMS work online and most transactions occur in real time – this means that the central database is updated immediately a transaction takes place. Building of indexes is usually a background activity and may take place overnight, so that, for example, a catalogue record created on one day may not be fully searchable until the next, although the record itself can be accessed immediately if its control number is known.

Cataloguing

Most academic libraries acquire the majority of their catalogue records from an external source, such as the British Library or their LMS supplier's shared database, as for example with Talis (in that particular case the service is known as *Talis Base*, and gives access to over 20 million records). The 'hit rate', that is the proportion of the required records supplied in this way, varies depending on the subject matter, the rarity of the material acquired and the time lag between publication and record requirement. The longer the lag the more likely that a record will be available from elsewhere.

All academic libraries in the UK now acquire records in MARC format, although the LMS will convert them into an internal format. Surveys of coverage are carried out by UKOLN at monthly intervals (Chapman, 1999) and indicate that academic libraries are able to acquire nearly 90% of their records in this way, the rate increasing to 94% six months after acquisition. The library needs to decide when a cut-off should be applied and the remaining records created in-house. With co-operative systems, such as Talis, member libraries contribute their locally generated records to the central, shared database, thus making them available to others and further reducing the need for local cataloguing.

It is particularly important with computer-based catalogues that good authority control is maintained, ensuring that standard headings – for example for authors or subjects – are always used. Authority control records may be created locally – in which case imported catalogue records will need to be modified to fit – or external data, such as Library of Congress authority files, may be used.

Ordering and acquisitions

The ordering/acquisitions module is designed to control all the processes involved in placing orders, sending these to suppliers, receiving books or other materials and controlling associated expenditure. The order record is in essence a skeleton catalogue record with additional purchasing and local information. Where suppliers undertake processing – such as spine labelling – the library will supply the classification number and main heading. Suppliers may also provide the MARC record, and it is now possible for them to upload this into the library's system remotely. Increasingly orders are sent electronically (using EDI systems) and reports from the supplier –

such as out of print, reprinting, price changes and other queries – are also transmitted to the LMS electronically where they may become available through the OPAC to the end-users.

The module must also undertake detailed fund accounting. Typically (see Chapter 7) academic libraries divide their book-funds into subject – effectively department – headings, with additional funds for general material, secondary publications such as abstracting and indexing services, etc. Book and journal expenditure may be handled separately. For each of these funds the LMS must maintain accurate records of amounts committed and amounts actually spent. These must take account of the university's financial year, carrying forward commitments from one year to the next, and crediting cancellations. Account must be taken of changes in the expected price, of discounts and of the effect of conversion rates on books priced in currencies other than sterling. Systems that are capable of sharing data with the university's main finance systems reduce the workloads of acquisitions staff in reconciling the two.

Serials

The serials module, designed to control the acquisition and handling of all types of serial, may at first glance appear to be a variation on the ordering/acquisitions module, but in fact there are very significant differences. Although both are concerned with acquiring materials from external suppliers (and therefore should share supplier data) and both have to control expenditure (and should therefore share access to budget files), the processes of controlling book and serial acquisition are quite different. Whereas a book is a one-off purchase, which is either received or not (even allowing for partial delivery of a multi-copy order), serials are received in a succession of instalments. Usually they are purchased on annual subscription, but the number of parts issued per year varies widely. The LMS should enable each subscription to be described by a 'prediction pattern', which is in essence a list of when each part is to be expected. As each issue is received – and an academic library could easily receive well over 100 issues each day – it needs to be checked off on the LMS. This enables the system to send alerts to staff when a part is missing – possibly because of a delay in publication, or because it has been lost in transit. The system should also generate claims to suppliers, preferably automatically.

Additional complications are that publishers sometimes produce an additional issue and often supply an annual index. All of these have to be controlled.

Electronic journal subscriptions are somewhat simpler to administer as a physical copy does not have to be received, but it is important that there is some monitoring of the subscriptions to ensure that issues are becoming available as expected.

Because the number of suppliers can be very large, many academic libraries use 'consolidation services', which handle the supply on behalf of libraries and deal with any claims that become necessary. The LMS then needs to be set up to reflect this practice.

Since libraries often bind volumes of serials, the LMS needs to be able to group issues into volumes and record them as 'at binding', subsequently changing the holdings record to identify the volume rather than each part as the basic unit. The holdings details in the bibliographic record can therefore become quite complex and very extensive.

OPAC

The OPAC or *Online Public Access Catalogue* provides the interface to enable library users to access the system. Modern LMS will invariably provide the OPAC through web pages delivered as part of the library's website, but the OPAC itself may be used as an interface to other resources beyond those held by the library. For example, it is now quite common to record web page URLs in catalogue records, so that by clicking on the URL the user can be taken directly to the web resource, wherever it may be.

OPACs normally provide a range of search options (author, author/title, title, classification, keyword, etc) and may enable Boolean searching. An issue in OPAC design is the level of complexity that should be provided – too complex and novice users will be unable to cope, but too simple and experienced users will be unable to perform complex searches to find the items they need. Although there was at one time a trend towards providing two modes – 'expert' and 'novice' – many systems now provide an interface which on the face of it is simple, and can operate effectively on single keywords, etc., but which will also accept and execute complex commands. Thus the interface appears simple to all users, but hides complex functionality and makes it available when needed.

The display of records on the OPAC can be equally problematic. Very few users want a display of the full MARC record, including all its tags, although some may – for example if they want to download the records into their own personal database, although this could raise copyright issues. The initial display needs to provide sufficient information to enable the relevance of items to be assessed, and hence is usually a list of abbreviated authors/titles with perhaps ten or 20 entries per page. Selecting any of these entries will lead to a display of the full record, with the shelfmark, holdings and status information – number of copies and which are out on loan. There may at this stage be an option to display the full MARC record.

When users have found items in which they are interested but which are out on loan, they should be able to go straight to placing a reservation. A further facility should be provided to enable them to check their own records – including the books they have out on loan, as a reminder, and those on which they have placed reservations. Access to this information must, of course, be secure and users will normally be required to enter a user name and password to gain access.

OPACs may be enhanced in a variety of ways. For example, in some systems clicking on the shelfmark is used to generate a display of the layout of the library with the correct location highlighted. An idea which might be borrowed from internet booksellers would be to display a thumbnail image of the book jacket alongside the bibliographic record, although this does not yet appear to have been implemented by UK academic libraries.

Circulation

The control of lending and related operations is perhaps the most critical function of the modern LMS. It has to be capable of handling very rapid transactions in which first a borrower number is used as the key to look up the borrower record on the system's central database and to carry out various validity and rights checks, and then each book number is used to perform a similar series of checks on the holdings record. Further validity checks are carried out, and – assuming all is in order – the loan transaction is recorded. This process is in fact considerably more complex than the typical commercial transaction logging system, such as those used at supermarket checkouts, yet the system response time has to be as quick. If it took only a few seconds to perform each check, each user with several books to borrow could be made to wait a minute or more, and the operator would process fewer than 60 borrowers an hour. Clearly throughput has to be much faster than that. Once the transaction has been authorized, the system must calculate the return date – and procedures must ensure that this matches the date stamped by staff on the date label in each book.

Academic libraries almost invariably use barcodes, which are read by hand-held or desk-mounted laser scanners, on books and borrower cards. Not only are barcodes quick to read but they incorporate a number of checking devices to ensure that the chances of misreading and using an incorrect number are remote. Other machine-readable technologies are sometimes used for borrower cards, including magnetic strips of the kind found on credit cards. These tend to be more effective where the card must also be used for other purposes, such as gaining entry to the library building, where swipe-card technologies have better first-time read rates.

As part of the book return function, the LMS must be capable of trapping books which are overdue, have outstanding reservations or are required for other purposes. Overdue charges, unfortunately termed 'fines' in most libraries, have to be calculated accurately. To do this the system needs to maintain a calendar which records dates when the library is open and closed, so that a charge is not made when books could not be returned. A possible complexity is that loan periods would not be extended purely because, say, a bank holiday occurred in the middle of the period: libraries differ in their attitude to the effects of this on overdue charges.

Where a returned book has a reservation against it, it must be put to one side, and the reserver informed. Again, this notification should be generated automatically by the LMS. Library staff should have the opportunity to change the order of the reservation queue where this is necessary – for example, if the library itself needs the book.

Other reasons for 'trapping' a book at the return point would include cases where a visual check is needed. For example, where a book is published with a CD-ROM or with maps library staff should check that they are present at the return point.

Renewals also need to be handled within the circulation system. Most academic libraries now allow self-service renewals, usually via the OPAC, although a limit on the number of times any one item may be renewed before it is physically checked by library staff is often applied.

Interlibrary loans

For many years interlibrary loan services have been operated using a different system to the main LMS, although this is now changing. Fretwell-Downing's VDX system, for example, offers self-service interlibrary loans alongside the LMS. Now that libraries are broadening the scope of interlibrary loans activities to include a wider variety of document delivery services – for both traditional and electronic documents – the integration of these functions will be the norm. Systems which handle these functions should ideally be compliant with the ILL Protocol Implementors Group (IPIG) profile and the associated ISO standards 10160 and 10161. Many systems, such as Ex-Libris' Aleph, are now compliant with these standards.

One of the reasons that the interlibrary loans module has been the last to be integrated is that it does not rely on the home library's catalogue. Instead it generates a request to another library for the supply of an item which, usually, it does not have in its own local stock. To achieve this, there needs to be a variety of mechanisms in place:

1   The home library needs to have pre-arranged procedures for making requests within either bilateral or, more usually, regional or national frameworks. All libraries operating within such agreements need to use common procedures.

2   There needs to be access to some form of catalogue of other libraries' holdings, in order to determine where requests should be sent. In fact, the UK is unusual in this regard in that some libraries bypass this requirement by sending all journals requests direct to the British Library's document supply services at Boston Spa without first checking the stock. BL can supply alternative locations if it cannot fulfil the request itself although it charges for this 'extended' service. In most other countries such a centralized, national service is not available.

3   There needs to be an agreed charging model in place since the supplying library needs to be compensated for its costs, including postage costs, etc. In the UK this is normally done by using British Library interlending forms as a kind of national interlending currency. Libraries operate accounts with BL itself and physical forms are not required for requests sent electronically.

The home library's systems need to be able to structure requests appropriately – at present this usually means the use of ARTTel which is the standard used by the BLDSC.

One of the disadvantages of not integrating interlibrary loans into the main LMS is that access to borrower data becomes more difficult. Integrated systems allow the borrower's status to be checked automatically – for example, a request might be denied to an undergraduate or to someone with overdue books. In integrated systems the status of the request – for example progress in fulfilling it – can also be shown online and checked by the requester through the OPAC.

A particular problem with interlibrary loans is that, where a photocopy is being supplied, the personal signature of the requester is required under copyright law. This means that, at least in theory and usually in practice, online requests are not permissible. This situation should start to change now that digital signatures are legally acceptable, although they are not yet widely used.

Management information

The LMS should be capable of providing statistical data to support management of the library. Performance measurement itself is discussed in Chapter 13, but one of the sources of the data needed by managers will be the library's own LMS. In fact the range of useful data may be quite limited, but it will be helpful to generate statistics, using the system's own report generator, on:

- the size and growth of the library's stock, subdivided by subject and with analyses of, for example, the age profile of the collection in terms of publication dates and acquisition dates
- acquisitions data, similarly subdivided, including analysis of acquisitions by academic department
- financial analyses, including the average prices of books and journals – this will be in addition to the ongoing reports on financial commitments and expenditure discussed above
- the number of loan transactions carried out each month, subdivided by user category (undergraduate, postgraduate, academic staff, external)

- the number of interlibrary loan transactions carried out subdivided into items requested from other libraries and items requested by other libraries.

Such statistics will be particularly useful when they are presented as time series so that comparisons can be made from month to month and from year to year. Many other analyses will be possible, but the real question will be the usefulness of each of these to management. It is thus preferable to consider not what the system can produce but what the manager actually needs.

Other functions

The LMS will usually be capable of supporting a number of other functions and processes in the library. For example, while few libraries still perform a complete stock check, the LMS will be able to produce lists of stock in particular areas, sorted into shelf order. A more sophisticated approach is to scan the barcodes of all the items on a particular run of shelving and input this data to the system. By allowing for items out on loan, being rebound, etc. the system can then produce a list of missing items – this needs further checking, of course, since some of those listed as missing will in fact have been in use within the library.

Increasingly, the LMS will be required to handle a broad range of transactions, such as e-payments, which arise through interaction with other systems. Such functions are under active development by all the major systems suppliers.

The IT systems strategic plan

For most academic libraries, the issue is no longer planning the implementation of an automated system *ab initio* but rather undertaking a long-term, planned replacement and enhancement strategy for existing systems. It is important that there should be an IT systems strategic plan, which should relate to the library's overall strategic plan (see Chapter 12), and should encompass all systems, not just the LMS. Many of the processes used in developing the strategic plan will be applicable also to the IT systems strategic plan.

The first stage in developing the IT systems strategic plan is to carry out an audit of existing systems to identify their strengths and weaknesses. This is not undertaken in a vacuum, for the staff responsible must be cognizant of the latest developments in the field and aware of the directions in which systems development is going – this is one of the reasons that it is important that system managers attend suitable conferences where presentations on new developments are made and where system suppliers are showcasing their products. Because major systems replacement takes place on a fairly long cycle (typically about once every five years), it may be wise to employ an expert consultant to help with this task.

The systems audit should provide a baseline from which planning can be developed. It will, for example, determine the quality of the library's database, the suitability of hardware such as PCs, and the compliance of existing systems to standards such as Z39.50 or ISO 10160. It will cover the performance of existing systems, including their reliability, the performance of the system supplier in maintaining the system and will identify any issues about the existing systems' capability of expansion.

Coupled with the audit there needs to be an appraisal of requirements – this is usually called a 'user requirements' definition, although the terminology can be confusing as to a system supplier it is the library which is the 'user'. In essence this definition tells potential suppliers *what* the library's systems should be able to do: it does not specify *how* those functions should be achieved. It is important that all library managers, and preferably all library staff, are consulted during this process and it is worth remembering that it is often library assistants, with their experience of front-line demands, who can best pinpoint shortcomings in systems. The information gleaned from this process is then used to create the first draft of the plan.

At this stage there needs to be careful consideration of the gaps: the ways in which current systems fail to deliver the functionality that the library requires. Some of these may be relatively trivial, while others may be quite fundamental. Furthermore, some may be easy to resolve, while others will require completely new systems. For example, if the library system is not ISO 10160 compliant, then this may be resolved by a new release of the current system from the supplier. If that is not available, and maybe not even on the horizon, then the only solution may be to replace the system entirely. Increasingly, the library system must be interoperable with a wide range of other internal and external systems, and the Plan must reflect these requirements.

The above processes will result in a number of possible strategies that could be pursued. These need to be costed in broad terms and the advantages and disadvantages of each assessed. For example, there may be a relatively cheap solution to one problem, but it may produce only a short-term solution. Careful discussion of the options by senior management, advised by the systems experts, is essential to identify the optimum solutions for the library. Once the broad solutions have been agreed it is necessary to return to the draft plan and start to identify the steps necessary to move from the user requirement and preferred solutions to systems definition. Clearly the amount of planning and procurement activity required will depend on the solutions being pursued: a completely new system will require far more effort than obtaining a new release of software from an existing supplier.

The plan itself must not be allowed to become out of date. Technological change means that it will be necessary to revisit and revise the plan frequently. Managing this process, and achieving up to date systems while providing the necessary level of continuity and stability which will enable staff to be efficient at their work, are major undertakings.

The system specification

On the assumption that significant changes are planned, it will be necessary to develop a system specification. Again this may be an area where a library will wish to employ an expert consultant, since the development of large system specifications is an infrequent task and requires quite detailed understanding of current developments in the field. It is sometimes tempting to develop a specification as a wish-list of everything that the library could possibly want in an ideal world, but this is usually counter-productive. It is always worth remembering that suppliers will base their responses on the products they have to sell: requiring them to undertake additional development work, perhaps to meet a rather arcane requirement which other customers will not want, should only be included after very careful consideration.

It is usual to prepare both a *functional specification* and a *technical specification*. The former states unambiguously and in considerable detail the functions which the system being procured should provide. It is usual to indicate which items are *essential* or *mandatory* and which are *desirable*, and suppliers should also be encouraged to specify, in their responses, any additional functions, not listed in the specification, which they can offer. The technical specification covers issues like the network infrastructure within which the new system must operate, technical standards requirements, security and system maintenance. It is very important that the specification is written in such a way that it is easy to judge whether each potential supplier conforms to each element, without leaving room for doubt. Framing specifications so that the supplier must respond 'yes' or 'no' to each requirement, rather than providing a general description, is a good way to achieve this.

System procurement

The procurement of a major library IT system is a complex exercise and is governed by a number of requirements and rules. The institution itself will have financial procedures which must be followed, and it may be that for a system costing, say, £250,000 the Vice-Chancellor will be the only authorized signatory for the process and the subsequent purchase. For large capital purchases it is mandatory for publicly funded bodies in the European Union, including universities, to advertise the procurement in the *Official Journal*. The rules for this are quite complex and it is essential that they are followed to the letter.

The system specification forms only part of the documentation required for a full procurement. It is usual to provide a pack of information, which is often termed the *operational requirement* which provides background information about the library, rules, timescales and other requirements for responses and for potential suppliers – these may include financial information about the company, its quality assurance processes, its track record in the market and so on – together with requirements for staff training, and the format in which tenders must be submitted.

The selection of the most appropriate system will require detailed and intensive work by an expert task group, who will have to read each proposal in detail and *interpret* the suppliers' offerings. Nothing should be taken at face value, and it is usual to draw up a shortlist of at least three suppliers. At this stage detailed discussions with existing customers of those suppliers, including site visits, are essential and the suppliers must be required to demonstrate their systems, including features about which there is any doubt. Once a preferred system has been identified, formal agreement on purchasing, including the legal contract, payment milestones etc., will usually be handled by the university's finance office.

System implementation

The most complex process of all is implementation, especially as the library will almost certainly be migrating from one system to another. Detailed planning of every stage will be required, including the transfer of data (borrower as well as catalogue data), staff training and user migration. The pre-implementation stage itself can be quite lengthy, and may involve parallel running of the old and new systems to prove the replacement before it goes live. A major system implementation may take well over a year to complete, such is its complexity, but there is now a depth of experience in the sector on which to draw (see Muirhead, 1997). In recent years there have also been moves to establish a standard core functional requirement which would ease the burden on both libraries and suppliers (see www.openrfp.com/).

Using IT to deliver services

Although academic libraries have used library management systems for many years, they now also use IT to deliver a wide range of other services direct to users. While there has been an element of this for a long time, for example through mediated online database searching, it is only during the last decade that IT-based delivery has become a major factor in service delivery as a whole.

It is worth remembering that the personal computer (PC) is little more than 25 years old, and that widespread use of networked PCs only became common in UK universities during the 1990s. Equally, the availability of high bandwidth connections between UK universities (the JANET network) is relatively recent - see Chapter 1. Finally, although the world wide web is now the delivery medium of choice for most information services, it has been in use by libraries for no more than ten years. As a result, the use of

IT to deliver library services, although it may appear well-established, is in fact still in its formative stages.

One of the major challenges for libraries is the *integration* of all these services. The user does not want to have to access a different interface every time he or she needs to use a different system: indeed the user very often would prefer not to know that a different system has been accessed. Given that libraries have developed OPACs as the key to delivery of their traditional services, it makes sense to examine how those systems can be used in a wider context. This may be achieved by a combination of two approaches:

- The library can use its home page on the web as the interface to its services, and provide from there a link to the OPAC as well as links to other services.
- The OPAC itself can be used as the front-end to a variety of services. For example, it might provide facilities to search a number of other libraries' OPACs, or it might be able to provide links to other kinds of 'data service'.

In Chapter 5, the range of external 'library' services was described. These include subject gateways, portals, specialist datasets, commercial services and so on. Some of these give direct access to information objects (such as electronic documents, web pages, and images in image banks) while others point to the locations of physical objects (books, printed journals, etc.). The need to integrate these has given rise to the concept of the 'hybrid library' as described in that chapter.

The problem for those responsible for academic library systems lies in the need to maintain control over this vast array of different systems and to ensure that they all interoperate and do so efficiently. It is beyond the scope of this book to discuss how this is achieved in any detail but it is appropriate to consider some of the approaches briefly.

First, all academic libraries now rely heavily on their web pages to provide the basic interface to their services. Users will usually encounter the home page first, and this should direct them to the various services available as well as to information about the library. Most libraries have developed sophisticated sites with large numbers of pages, and the organization and maintenance of the website is thus a major task. It is important that pages are checked regularly for broken links (software is available to do this) and that usage is monitored to ensure that heavily used pages are easily accessible. Care is also needed to ensure that the search engine, almost invariably provided as part of the site, is working correctly, perhaps using metadata provided in the page headers. Issues like accessibility also need attention (see Chapter 11).

As well as general information and access to general services, most academic libraries provide subject-specific pages from which users can link to sources which have been assessed as being of particular relevance and of good quality. Some of these links may be to the national gateways such as SOSIG and PsiGate, while others might be to commercial gateway services, services run by professional bodies, and so on.

Most OPACs are now accessed from a front-end web page or portal which enables searching of multiple sources – whether this page is provided by the library management system or by another software package. The user is thus able to search from the front-end in a number of different ways. From the library systems point of view, the portal therefore needs to be able to provide a number of functions:

1   Users should be able simply to search the local library catalogue if that is what they want, perhaps because they are physically in the building or intend to visit it.

2   Users should also be able to search a range of catalogues, either by selecting from a list displayed on a web page or by specifying a term or condition which the software can interpret and then use to automatically select relevant catalogues. Where this 'clump' is created by software the process is called *dynamic clumping*: refer to Chapter 5 for descriptions of the eLib clump (also known as large-scale resource discovery) projects. In this way, the user could search, say, all the local library catalogues at once, or all catalogues of specialist libraries in his or her subject.

3   The system should be able to handle different types of source, for example local and remote library catalogues, remote data services (such as those provided by the JISC data centres), commercial electronic journals and so on.

4   The software must be able to present the results in a 'sensible' way. For example, it would be helpful to sort them into some kind of order and

to remove duplicate entries. It would be useful to be able to flag those entries where the user has limited access rights, and maybe not to display those where the user has no access rights at all.

5   It must be possible for the systems librarian to add new sources (targets) to the list of those that can be searched without having to provide amendments or updates to the searching software. This is one of the most difficult issues to resolve, since it implies that all the sources must use the same standards for describing items and for responding to automated queries. This issue is referred to as *interoperability* and was discussed briefly in Chapter 5.

A further major issue for the library is that of authenticating and authorizing users. In the days when services were delivered in a building it was relatively easy to insist that each user register by completing a form and being given a membership ticket. But when services start to be delivered beyond the building, and when some of those services carry conditions as to who may use them, things become much more complicated. First of all it is necessary to be able to *authenticate* users, that is to verify who they are and to be sure that they are who they say they are. In the past this has been achieved by giving each borrower a membership card, often with a photograph, and requiring it to be shown and checked at some service points – many academic libraries have restricted admission to the building in this way. With online systems the issue becomes much more complicated. Usually it is handled by issuing each user with a *user name* and *personal identification number* (PIN), which are input at an initial log-in screen. However, some services – most notably the OPAC – may be provided on open access at some or all locations.

Where some kind of access restrictions have to be applied – perhaps because of the terms of a commercial contract, which may strictly limit access to members of the institution – it is necessary to *authorize* users as well as authenticating them. (It is worth noting that terminology in this field is often used inconsistently, and 'authentication' is sometimes used to include 'authorization' processes.) Authorization requires a process whereby the user's rights can be checked.

In some circumstances authorization can take place without authentication. For example, if use of a resource is limited to members of the institution, a common way to provide authorization is for the software to check the IP address of the workstation from which the request originates. If this is one of the range used by machines on-campus, access can be granted without knowing who the individual user is. Unfortunately, although this has been a popular way to authorize access in the past, it falls down once users start to demand off-campus access. Most home access, for example, will be via an Internet Service Provider (ISP) which allocates an IP address dynamically as and when a user connects. There is thus no way of using IP addressing to grant access in these circumstances.

Another way of granting access is to check the user's user name and password each time access to a particular resource is required. While this was a reasonable procedure when there were only a handful of resources available, it becomes unwieldy once a large number are potentially accessible. First an individual user name and password has to be issued to each user, or group of users, for each resource. Secondly mechanisms are needed to maintain those records, dealing with lost passwords, imposing requirements for frequent changes to passwords to protect security, removing user names when users leave the institution, and so on. Thirdly, a proliferation of passwords becomes impossible for users to handle. All that happens is that users change as many of their identities as possible to the same password and, because this is not always possible, end up having to write down a list. It then becomes quite common to see a list of user names and passwords taped to the workstation and available for all to see!

What is needed is a *single sign-on* process which enables the user to be authenticated at the first screen, and then for software to handle onward authorization as and when necessary. This then becomes a much more efficient process for all concerned. To make it happen, what is needed is first, agreement on standards and protocols, so that all target systems can understand the authorization system, and secondly, a database system in which are held the user names and associated access privileges. The ATHENS system, which was the first attempt to implement such a system in UK higher education, was described in Chapter 5.

ATHENS is not a perfect solution, although it represents a significant advance for higher education in the UK. Among its deficiencies are its limited facilities for holding data about users, which is needed if services are to be personalized and meaningful data on service usage is to be gathered. It is likely that an enhanced system will be implemented in due course, perhaps incorporating the use of digital signatures and probably based on the

Shibboleth model (see http://shibboleth.internet2.edu/docs/internet2-mace-shibboleth-introduction-200404.pdf). A particular issue will be the interoperability of higher education's system with broader e-commerce developments.

Conclusion

The library management system provides the essential infrastructure which enables the modern academic library to deliver its services. Because ICTs are pervasive in libraries and in the systems and services they use, the infrastructure is complex and needs constant updating. Integration with other institutional systems and those provided externally is vital. Where in the past the major concern was to control the library's own stock, the LMS must now integrate heterogeneous services and present them in a meaningful and accessible way to users. A particular issue is the authentication and authorization of each user to ensure that services are accessed only by those entitled to use them, but this needs to be done in a user-friendly manner which does not place endless barriers in the way of the individual users. Each library needs to define its own IT infrastructure requirements, taking all of these issues into account and reflecting its particular service mix, using an IT systems strategic plan to guide development.

References

Chapman, A. (1999) Availability of Bibliographic Records for the UK Imprint, *Journal of Documentation,* 55 (1), 6–15 (reports, www.ukoln.ac.uk/bib-man/surveys/bnbmarc/summary.html/)

Muirhead, G. (ed.) (1997) *Planning and Implementing Successful System Migrations*, Library Association Publishing.

Further reading

Cohn, J. M., Kelsey, A. L. and Fiels, K. M. (2002) *Planning for Integrated Systems and Technologies: a how-to-do-it manual for librarians*, 2nd edn, revised by David Salter, Facet Publishing.

The websites of the major LMS suppliers are at:

Dynix
   www.dynix.com/
Endeavour
   www.endinfosys.com/
Ex Libris
   www.exlibrisgroup.com/
Fretwell-Downing Informatics
   www.fdgroup.com/fdi/welcome/index.html
Geac
   www.library.geac.com/
Innovative Interfaces
   www.iii.com/
Sirsi
   www.sirsi.co.uk/
Talis
   www.talis.com/

11
Services

Introduction

In earlier chapters, frequent references have been made to the services which academic libraries offer to their users. In this chapter we bring together these different aspects of service so as to take an overview of the portfolio the library offers. This also provides an opportunity to look at some of the cross-service issues which need to be addressed if a coherent library service is to be presented to all users.

Most academic libraries offer some specialist services which are designed to meet the needs of particular user groups or which relate to particular parts of the stock. Such services must be designed to meet local requirements and conditions, but again they must present a coherent approach to the users.

Study: the learning environment

Many library users regard the library primarily as a place to study. This is particularly true of students, who may have nowhere else suitable to go, or may find the environment offered by the library more conducive to study than their own, perhaps noisy or uncomfortable, accommodation.

A successful study environment is a combination of many different factors. In Chapter 1 we examined the increasingly varied approaches to learning being taken in higher education. We looked at the different needs of different types of user in Chapter 4 and at the physical environment in Chapter 9. In a number of earlier chapters the needs of users for access to IT-based services was considered.

While the individual study carrel or table, together with its IT-enabled equivalent, remains a central requirement for most academic libraries, there is also demand for group study spaces which are set out to enable team working. These may require a large table around which the team can sit, together with presentation facilities such as a whiteboard, overhead projector or flipchart.

A useful parallel for these requirements can be found in office architecture, where the need is frequently for highly flexible spaces. Some of these will be meeting rooms for discussions, task groups or formal committees; some will be individual desks, but often provided for 'hot desking' so that they can be used by anyone in the firm or by visiting clients; some will be larger open-plan areas designed to encourage interaction between individuals; some open-plan areas will provide screening for semi-private working areas. Shared facilities such as photocopiers will be adjacent to each group of work places. Managers – the academic library equivalent might be the advisory desk or perhaps a desk for tutors – will be adjacent to work areas. There will be at least one large space where staff can be brought together – the equivalent might be a large lecture room.

While this model is currently useful, new forms of learning environment are emerging, an issue which will be discussed in Chapter 15 and which will require librarians to re-evaluate the physical learning spaces and services provided.

Reference and enquiry services

The academic library's ability to offer authoritative advice is one of its hallmarks. In particular, the facility for users to secure help with their information enquiries is one of the 'bedrock' services which users value and exploit. In a time of mass higher education this type of service may be difficult and expensive to maintain, but it makes the difference for many users between inability to find the required information in the mass of sources which face them and successful exploitation of those resources. While part of the reference service may be provided electronically, human face-to-face contact remains a vital component.

The task of providing this type of service is complex and draws on a wide range of skills. To begin with, it is vitally important that library staff have the interpersonal communication skills to be effective in this role. This means the ability to listen carefully to users and to draw out from them their real needs. It also means the ability not just to find an answer to the query but in so doing to help the user to learn how to resolve similar queries for themselves in the future – in other words, the reference/enquiry service should be a learning opportunity for the user. These interpersonal skills must sit alongside highly developed knowledge of the literature – and increasingly of the technology used to deliver that literature – of the subject in question.

Enquiries from users can take many forms. For example they may be:

- directional, asking 'where is' a particular library collection, subject literature, or simply a facility
- factual, asking for a discrete piece of information, such as the boiling point of a chemical
- library policy or procedure, such as opening hours, reservation procedures or loan periods
- skills-related, such as how to use a microform reader or the OPAC
- known-item searching, such as how to check whether an item, bibliographic details of which are known, is in the library's stock
- subject, such as how to find information on any particular topic.

This last category is of course the most complex, and may require the librarian to refer the user on to a specialist in that subject.

Reference and enquiry services may be delivered in many different ways. Typically, the library will provide one or more enquiry desks – some libraries have centralized these to save on staffing costs while others maintain separate enquiry points for each major subject area. Converged services may offer a converged enquiry point, or may decide to keep 'library' and 'IT' enquiry services separate, perhaps because the skills and knowledge required of those who staff them are different. Increasingly, reference and enquiry services are provided remotely through e-mail or the web, perhaps using an 'Ask a Librarian' service. In these cases the lack of immediacy and limited opportunity to explore enquiries more fully makes it imperative that the service is well managed and provides opportunities for feedback and iteration. The relationship between enquiry and reference services and information skills training is clearly close, and the planning of both needs to take place hand-in-hand (see also Chapter 4).

It is important to remember that users will see any interaction with *any* library staff as an opportunity to pose enquiries. So shelvers will be approached for help by users having difficulty finding a book on the shelves, while issue desk staff will be asked quite complex, subject-related questions as an incidental to issuing books. It is therefore important that all staff have basic training in handling enquiries and know when to pass the enquiry on to a more experienced member of staff.

The reference and enquiry service will be supported by printed and web-based guides, ranging from a general library guide with floor-plans through worksheets on using a particular service to subject-specific guides to the literature of a particular field. A useful way of monitoring the effectiveness of such guides is to monitor the questions being asked of the enquiry service, and where necessary to revise a guide or produce a new one as a means of answering frequent queries. As well as making such guides freely available, reference and enquiry staff should hand them to users to help answer specific queries.

Access to information

We have already examined many of the individual services which together provide users with access to information sources which may be of interest to them. If we assume that the academic library will be 'hybrid', as defined in Chapter 3, for the foreseeable future, then some of the information required will be made available from printed and other 'hard copy' sources held by the library itself, some of the same kinds of media will be borrowed from elsewhere for users, and some will be made available electronically – in which case users may not be aware of the source.

Providing a 'seamless' service which integrates all of these sources is a major challenge. Academic librarians in the future will need to pay particular attention to this issue, especially as their responsibility is to ensure that the sources supplied are those which are both the most effective (i.e. most closely meet the users' information needs) and most efficient (i.e. are supplied as economically as possible, taking all costs into account). Given that budgets will continue to be under great pressure, understanding the factors which affect the balance between holdings – buying a book which is expected to be used a number of times – against access – purchasing the right to use an information object each time it is needed or for a limited period – will be of great importance.

Lending services remain at the core of academic library provision. It is usual to operate a number of different loan periods, depending on the popularity of items and on user status, although a number of items will be available only for reference – this is commonly the case for journals. Typically, the main stock may be borrowable by academic staff for a term and by students for four weeks. A medium loan period of a week is common for items in relatively heavy demand. Material in very heavy demand may be placed in the short-loan collection, where loan periods will usually be for a few hours or overnight. In order to guarantee fast turnaround of this material, it is often either held on closed access or in a separate area with its own security controls, and charges for late return will usually be heavy.

Subject-based services

The subject specialist approach to service delivery was described in Chapter 6 in the context of library staff roles. This covered the major responsibilities of such staff, usually to a faculty or group of cognate departments, for liaison, stock selection, information skills tuition, and so on. However, it is sometimes desirable to supplement these common services with specific services tailored to particular subject needs. Two examples are given in this section, with some observations on the issues they raise.

Art and design

Whereas in most subjects the printed word has been dominant, in art and design – and all the related disciplines – it is images that are paramount. Academic libraries have generally struggled to meet these requirements, partly because copyright law has made it particularly difficult for libraries to develop the image collections they need. The traditional art and design library has tried to overcome such barriers by developing specialist collections, including:

- slide collections, which have often been academic staff's preferred image format
- collections of printed images, sometimes – as with fashion, for example – created by taking cuttings from magazines and newspapers

- exhibition catalogues, which are often the only definitive source of information
- specialist books, periodicals, videos, etc.

Issues which arise from developing these kinds of collection include those of cataloguing, control of access and control of borrowing. In each case different procedures and processes are needed from those used in a 'normal' library setting. Electronic collections, especially of high resolution images, are now of increasing importance.

Law

While law uses textual information, much of its required material is set out in formal statutes, law reports and the like. In other words, the *raw material* of the law is its textual material, while the commentary on that material forms yet another literature. This means that for a lawyer, the library is the equivalent of the chemist's laboratory and a comprehensive collection of the main legal materials is essential. A collection which is not comprehensive - in the sense of providing a copy of all the major primary literature - is of little use. In the UK, where legal precedent is all-important, law reports (which describe judgments in the courts) are as important as the statutes themselves. Much, but by no means all, of this material is now available electronically (e.g. *All England Direct*, providing access to the *All England Law Reports* from 1936).

In addition to this primary literature, academic lawyers will require a collection of secondary literature, both in the sense of textbooks and other commentaries on the law and in the sense of finding and alerting tools. Increasingly, the latter will be electronic and services such as LEXIS are now virtually indispensable.

Archival and special collections

Many academic libraries contain special collections, usually of a historical nature, which require different treatment from that provided for mainstream collections and services. Such collections have many different origins: some represent the original foundation collections, possibly centuries old; some developed because of special interests of members of the academic staff; some were gifted to the university by benefactors; some may have been purchased in their entirety.

Normally, special collections are housed separately from the main collections and they are more likely to be provided with carefully monitored physical environments, including temperature and humidity control, to prevent damage, and security arrangements to prevent theft. The bibliographical description of items in such collections may be very much more detailed than would be the case with the main collections: for example, pagination, illustrations, bindings, etc. may be described in detail. Valuable items may be scanned and made available as digitized images, both to generate interest in the collection and to enable some use to be made of surrogates, although scholars will usually want to examine originals. Preservation and conservation issues were discussed in Chapter 8.

The detailed management of archival collections, whatever their origins, requires specialist skills and is a subject which goes beyond the scope of this book.

Users with special needs

Mention was made in Chapter 4 of the need to consider service delivery from the viewpoint of users with special needs. In this section we look at some of the ways in which that can be achieved. It is important not to make the assumption that attention to the needs of one group of disabled users means that others have been considered. The library which claims to have resolved disability access problems because it has provided a ramp at the entrance has clearly not thought through the issue from the point of view of a blind person, whose access may even have been made more difficult! The general principle should always be that of 'Design for All'.

In the UK the 1995 Disability Discrimination Act placed obligations on all organizations to ensure accessibility and was supplemented by the Special Educational Needs and Disability Act 2001 which refers specifically to educational provision. Universities and colleges must take all reasonable steps to ensure that disabled people are not discriminated against. Under the legislation, both institutions and individuals have responsibilities, so it is imperative that all staff are fully trained in the implications. These responsibilities apply to staff, to third parties and to students - prior to SENDA students were outside the scope of the Act for most purposes.

The kinds of issues which should be addressed by library staff include:

- physical access to all parts of the library building
- information about the service (available in various media, including audio and, preferably, braille, so as to make it accessible to all)
- transcription services if the major role of the organization is in providing information
- induction loops wherever the spoken word is used
- audiovisual fire alarms
- properly trained staff.

The JISC Legal Information Service provides detailed advice on the application of the legislation. The legal issues surrounding web site accessibility have been described in some detail by Sloan (2001) while TechDis offers advice and resources. Craven (2001) has researched the ways in which students with visual impairment search the web.

For academic libraries, the best strategy is usually to integrate services for disabled users into the mainstream service as far as possible, and to try to ensure that such users are not singled out. However, it is sometimes desirable to offer enhanced levels of service – an extended loan period would be an obvious example – and this may mean providing a special ID card. Staff should be careful not to draw attention to the disability when this kind of procedure is necessary.

Blind and visually impaired people

Blind and visually impaired people face many difficulties when accessing library services. Not only do they have problems of physical access, such as the placing of doorways and barriers which have to be negotiated, but they may be unable to read signs and guides. Even more importantly, the basic media which libraries use are not conducive to non-visual access. Not only does this include print-on-paper, but the electronic media are becoming increasingly visual in content and presentation – web pages contain more and more images, often not just for decoration but to provide information.

There are two complementary approaches to making information sources accessible to blind and visually impaired people. First, it is possible to provide services which enable existing resources to be transcribed into a suitable format: for example, a chapter of a book could be transcribed into braille. A surprisingly large number of visually impaired people can be helped simply by providing a magnifier or a large PC screen. Secondly, tools can be provided which enable the 'native' format, usually electronic, to be read satisfactorily by a non-visual output device. So, for example, a *screen reader* can be used to turn the contents of a workstation display into audio output. It is extremely important that the original object has been designed with this kind of usage in mind, and the World Wide Web Consortium's Web Accessibility Initiative (WAI) has issued guidelines for web developers on this matter.

Deaf and hearing-impaired users

While most deaf and hearing-impaired users are able to read text and view images – although the needs of deafblind people who cannot must not be ignored – they still need special consideration from library staff. Obviously, audio resources will create problems, and video will be inaccessible unless it is captioned. Text telephones are available which enable a deaf person to type and/or receive back typed messages on a small screen, and it is good practice for academic libraries to install at least one. A particular issue is whether deaf users can be alerted to emergencies, library closure, etc. – a visual fire alarm system may be needed, and the procedure for closing the library in the evening designed to ensure that deaf and hearing-impaired people are made aware of what is happening.

A serious problem can occur for deaf people because their disability is so easily unrecognized. Staff must be trained *not* to assume that everyone coming to enquiry or issue desks has good hearing – it is highly embarrassing for a deaf person to discover that the person serving them is shouting at them and in the process announcing their disability to the world. Since many deaf people can lip-read, training staff to speak clearly and observing a few other elements of good practice – such as facing the person being served, avoiding standing in front of a bright light or window, and keeping your hands away from your face – can make all the difference. Training one or two staff in sign language is a useful strategy.

Users with motor disabilities

The most obvious problems for users with motor disabilities are those of access - access to the building itself and access within the building. Many of these issues are to do with building design, such as the provision of ramped access, consideration of how users with walking aids or in wheelchairs will negotiate doors, and ensuring that a lift is available to every floor. The width of aisles, especially between bookshelves, should be sufficient to take a standard wheelchair wherever possible. Users with motor disabilities may need accessible reader places - for example, they may need additional width to accommodate a wheelchair. They may also need help from staff, for example to take books down from high shelves.

Conclusion

The core services of the academic library include the provision of a learning environment, reference and enquiry services and access to information sources. However, each library must tailor its precise service mix to the needs of the users it serves. In some universities particular subjects will pose particular requirements - as with art and design or law. Others will have special collections, and must take their archival responsibilities seriously. For all libraries, accessibility for all should be a guiding principle, with the needs of users with disabilities given careful thought and particular attention.

References

Craven, J. (2001) Understanding the Searching Process for Visually Impaired Users of the Web, *Ariadne*, **26**,
www.ariadne.ac.uk/issue26/craven/intro.htm

Sloan, M. (2001) Web Accessibility and the DDA, *The Journal of Information, Law and Technology (JILT)*, issue 2,
http://elj.warwick.ac.uk/jilt/01-2/sloan.html.

Further reading

For case studies of integrated library services refer to Hanson, T. and Day, J. (1998) *Managing the Electronic Library: a practical guide for information professionals*, Bowker-Saur.

World Wide Web Consortium (W3C) *Web Accessibility Initiative* www.w3.org/WAI/

Organizations serving the needs of disabled people in UK higher education include:

JISC Legal Advisory Service, disability advice
www.jisclegal.ac.uk/disability/accessibility.htm
RNIB: Royal National Institute for the Blind
www.rnib.org.uk/
RNID: Royal National Institute for the Deaf
www.rnid.org.uk/
NLB: National Library for the Blind
www.nlbuk.org/
TechDis
www.techdis.ac.uk/

12
Management

Introduction

In earlier chapters mention has been made of a number of management issues and management approaches. The purpose of this chapter is to consider academic library management as a whole. First, however, it is useful to provide some definitions of the terms used.

Management is concerned, first and foremost, with the organization and direction of different kinds of resources for specific purposes. Clearly it is important that these purposes are known and are explicit, otherwise the manager will not know which direction to take. At the highest level of formal statements, the organization should have a *mission statement*: this is a statement of why it exists in the first place - what is its purpose? The mission statement itself is built on two things: a vision of what the organization could be and wants to be, and an understanding of its values. For academic libraries, because they are part of larger organizations, it is vital that the vision, values and mission are tied closely to those of the parent university. For example, if the university is primarily a teaching institution, the library should reflect this. On the other hand, if the university is concerned primarily with research, and especially where the library has historic collections of great importance, the vision, values and mission will be very different. A discussion of how mission statements are developed, and examples of some university library mission statements, can be found in Brophy (1991).

Strategic aims will be derived from the mission statement. These are broad statements which set out long-term goals for the library to achieve - for example, an aim might be 'to ensure all members of the university have good information skills'. At the next level, each aim will have one or more objectives associated with it - these are shorter term goals, which will be expressed in more precise language: an example might be 'to deliver a library induction session to 95% of new undergraduate students each year'.

It will be seen that as one becomes more precise with mission, aims and then objectives, so it becomes easier to devise clear measurements or indicators of achievement. From a knowledge of the total number of new undergraduate students enrolled in the institution and the library's own records of those attending induction sessions, it is simple to calculate whether the 95% threshold has been reached. It is less easy to know whether or not all members of the university have good information skills, since they may acquire these in many different ways and there may be differences of opinion as to what constitutes 'good' in this context. It is yet more difficult to measure achievement of the mission itself - indeed it can be argued that the mission is not 'achievable' in this sense, since it is always a target on the horizon. In the next chapter we will return to the issue of how the performance of the library as a whole may be measured.

Responsibility for achieving the mission, aims and objectives of the library will be devolved amongst the staff. To achieve this it is necessary to be explicit about management responsibilities. The university librarian or equivalent manager is responsible for ensuring that the library is pursuing a clear mission and strategy, and for ensuring that there are adequate, which is not to say generous, resources to enable that to be done. He or she is the *strategic* manager. At the next level, one or more deputy librarians, or the equivalent managers, will be responsible for the operation of the library on a day to day basis: they are the *operational* managers. Sometimes these responsibilities will be allocated on the basis of functional divisions of the library (for example, acquisitions, collection management, reader services) or they may occur on a cross-functional basis such as personnel, finance and so on. There is then a level of *tactical* management. Here the heads of units - such as the service desk or interlibrary loans - will be responsible for managing operations on a continuing basis, for example for ensuring adequate staff numbers are allocated to each duty for every minute that the library is open.

Among the most important managerial tasks at each of these levels are *leadership* and *co-ordination*. Leadership is a difficult quality to define, but in essence it consists of the ability to articulate and share a vision of how things can and should be and then to enthuse staff to achieve that vision. This is true whether we are talking of the strategic level, where the vision may be of a world-class digital research library, or the tactical level, where the vision may be of fast turnround of requests coupled with friendly service to each user.

Co-ordination is important because it is essential that all managers work together to achieve common aims. It is disastrous if managers are simply interested in their own particular areas and spare no thought for the effects of what they do on the rest of the organization. Faced with staff cuts, the temptation may be to try to pass workloads onto other sections but the accomplished manager will view the problem from a wider perspective and propose solutions which will minimize the effects on the library as a whole and on its users.

Finally, it is important to remember that the academic library is managed as part of a larger organization. It cannot invent all its own procedures to suit itself but will have to operate within the policies and procedures, such as those for finance and personnel, which the university lays down. More positively, its achievements can contribute to those of the institution as a whole.

Planning

Planning is an activity in which all managers must engage. Strategic planning concerns the future of the library as a whole while more specific plans may be drawn up for individual services, or to guide a major development such as the selection and implementation of a new library management system. Corrall (1994) has described strategic planning as 'a process in which purposes, objectives and plans are formulated, and then implemented . . . relating an organisation to its changing market opportunities'.

In essence the development of plans involves assessing both the external environment – which for an academic library means both its parent university and the broader information world – and the organization itself, and setting down directions which will be taken. Many techniques exist to help with environmental analysis – Corrall (1994) suggests the use of PEST (Politics, Economics, Society, Technology) which provides a structure within which the major factors are grouped for analysis. For example, a library might analyse both local and national political factors, the impact of economic factors such as exchange rates and rates of inflation, changes in society's expectations of libraries and the impacts of technological change. Coupled with this, SWOT (Strengths, Weaknesses, Opportunities, Threats) analysis - which focuses on the existing strengths and weaknesses of the organization, the opportunities it has to develop and the threats to its existence and prosperity - can be used to analyse the internal situation and relate it to likely trends outside. Having done this, a number of *planning assumptions* can be stated, making explicit the expectations of the planners about future trends.

A useful process is then to write down and discuss a series of *scenarios*, which are in essence descriptions of or even stories about the future as it might be if particular directions are taken. Some of these scenarios can be fairly outrageous, since the purpose is to stimulate thought about what is desirable - for example, an interesting scenario for a modern academic library to debate might be based around a future without books.

Although there are many formal planning systems available, most academic libraries will use processes which are agreed in their university, if only because the library's plans must fit with those of the parent institution. The *process* of planning must be clearly understood, and the role of all participants - which should include all library staff, since all have a contribution to make - made explicit. The university will itself develop strategic plans concerning finance, the physical estate, staffing, academic development and many other issues. The library's plans must both contribute to and draw upon these wider considerations. It is also worth noting that the library's plans can be a very effective means of communicating concerns, intentions and problems to the wider community.

The library's strategic plan will set out the general direction it is expected to take over the longer term - which because of the rate of change usually means no more than three years. There will also be plans concerned with specific aspects of service: the need for an *IT systems strategic plan* was considered in Chapter 10, but as indicated above a number of others may be needed.

The days of fixed plans which had to be adhered to come what may are long past and it is now accepted that plans must be implemented flexibly, taking account of changed circumstances, new opportunities, etc. Nevertheless, the plan provides the agreed strategy which will be adopted, and changes to it must themselves be agreed.

The implementation of a plan is itself a complex process. A first step may be to develop a series of action plans, which set out precise targets to be achieved by a fixed deadline and state clearly who is responsible for their achievement. Where the plan concerns a particular project, project management tools, such as PRINCE2, can be used – these break the project into work packages and tasks, allocate roles, responsibilities and resources and track progress against the plan and in particular against planned 'milestones' i.e. points where sub-tasks should have been completed. More generally, it is useful to identify a series of *critical success factors* (CSFs) which can be measured regularly. Progress against the plan can then be charted against these factors.

The management of change

Because, as we have already noted, change is virtually constant in higher education and in librarianship, one of the library manager's most important tasks is to ensure that change is *managed* and does not just 'happen'. To achieve this it is important to recognize that resistance to change is not born of a wish to be obstructive – or at least, not usually! – but because of deeply held beliefs about the values which change may destroy. It is therefore essential that there is a credible vision of the future which change is intended to bring about, and that steps are taken to gain commitment from all stakeholders both to the vision itself and to the path being pursued to achieve it. No-one would pretend that this is easy.

A useful approach which has been adopted in industry and commerce is centred round the idea of a 'learning organization' or 'learning company' (Pedler, Burgoyne and Boydell, 1991). The major elements of this approach are:

1   A *learning approach to strategy*, so that the process of formulating policies and strategies is itself structured as a learning process.
2   *Participative policy-making*, which enables the views and interests of all the stakeholders to be brought into the equation and encourages participation from across the whole organization.
3   *'Informating'*, which means using information throughout the organization to help members understand what is happening, and not for punishment or reward, trying to avoid the situation where only some people are 'in the know'. Information and information

technology are thus the 'oil' which enables the organization to move forward its understanding and hence its actions.

4 *Formative accounting and control*, to enable people to learn from financial reports and to adjust their decision-making and actions through this learning process. Accountants and financial officers see their role as consultants offering advice rather than 'scorekeepers and bean-counters'.

5 *Internal exchange*, which emphasizes the need for co-operative relationships between sections of the organization.

6 *Reward flexibility*, which encourages openness in reward systems and involvement of staff throughout the organization in the determination of such systems, while the need for different rewards to reflect the different contributions that people make is recognized.

7 *Enabling structures*, for example through seeing appraisal schemes as opportunities for identifying learning and development needs rather than as a mechanism for reward or punishment. Structures and procedures are necessary, but they should be reviewed regularly.

8 *Boundary workers as environmental scanners*, so that all staff, but especially those with jobs at the interface between the company and the outside world, see part of their work as bringing information and intelligence back into the organization for the use of everyone.

9 *Inter-company learning* which could include meetings with competitors as well as with suppliers and customers, to learn and to share ideas, information and developments. Techniques such as benchmarking (see chapter 13) are used as part of this process.

10 *A learning climate*, in which mistakes are seen as learning opportunities, and time is set aside to examine and discuss current practice, so as to engage in continuous improvement.

11 *Self-development opportunities for all*, including the external stakeholders. Everyone is given opportunities, and provided with resources, to undertake self-development.

This approach is expanded in Brophy and Coulling (1996), from which the above outline has been adapted.

Management style

Organizations differ widely in the ways in which they are managed. This is not just a matter of the effectiveness of their managers, but reflects genuine differences in style which derive from a range of sources. These include:

1   The history of the organization and the style which it has inherited.
2   The style which is 'imposed' or 'encouraged' by the parent organization. For example, some universities have a very egalitarian style in which all staff, and sometimes students, are consulted widely. Others operate a more authoritarian or hierarchical style, in which senior staff from the Vice-Chancellor downwards determine what will be done. Sometimes these styles are hidden and the reality may be opposite of what is stated – many organizations claim to welcome participation in decision-making when in fact they operate quite the opposite practice.
3   The personalities of the managers, and whether they are comfortable with a particular style. Some library directors like to direct!
4   Conceptual styles: the librarian who believes strongly in the concept of the networked library may, perhaps unconsciously, demand a 'high tech' style from his or her staff and this may colour the whole management of the library.

Quality management

There are many approaches to management and many schools of thought about management theory and practice. It can be difficult to reconcile all these ideas and schools of thought into a coherent overall approach. To some extent this is a matter of preference, but one approach which has become popular in recent years, not only in libraries, is *quality management* (Brophy and Coulling, 1996). As the name suggests it focuses first and foremost on the quality of the product or service being offered and, as noted briefly at the start of Chapter 4, it concentrates on ensuring that services meet user needs. Quality assurance is a major issue in higher education in general, and very considerable resources are expended to ensure that the standard of research and teaching in institutions is acceptable. Taking a quality management approach to library services therefore aligns the library closely with institutional concerns.

In brief, quality management focuses first and foremost on two issues: customer satisfaction and continuous improvement. Deriving originally from Japanese and then American business management, quality management became a dominant approach in the UK during the 1990s, and evoked considerable interest among librarians. Under the terminology of *total quality management* (TQM) it brings together a series of issues in a coherent manner, addressing:

- the need for each organization to be clear about its *purpose*: what its mission, aims and objectives really are
- having a consistent *focus on customer needs* throughout all of the organization's operations
- senior managers' responsibility for providing *leadership*, including a *vision* of the organization's future
- *commitment* by all employees to the organization
- the use of *teamwork* to bring employees together to work on issues and developments, using the strengths that each member of the team can bring to the task in hand
- *involvement* of all staff in decision-making and communication – a participative style
- having *systematic processes* in place so that services are delivered consistently and users know what to expect
- good *resource management* with resources understood to encompass not just financial resources but people, buildings, materials and knowledge
- good *relationships with suppliers*, so that those on whom the organization depends for its raw materials – in library terms book suppliers, periodicals agents, data services etc. – are committed to the organization's goals and supported in their efforts to supply the right materials at the right time
- *benchmarking*, which in essence is a process of comparing yourself against the best in your field, understanding how they operate and seeking to apply that approach in a suitable way to one's own organization
- *monitoring performance*, so that the managers know how well the organization is performing and can take action both to correct problems and to pursue excellence

- *training and development* of all staff so that they are competent in all the tasks they are asked to perform, knowledgeable about the organization and all its services or products, and understand the ethos and style of the organization
- understanding of how the organization *impacts on its environment* – in library terms this could be interpreted as the broader role within the local community, or could refer to the contribution that the library makes to society as a whole, perhaps through the preservation of recorded knowledge.

The European Foundation for Quality Management awards a series of quality awards each year to companies which are judged to be offering outstanding quality as defined by its *Excellence Model* (European Foundation for Quality Management, 2004). It is an interesting exercise to examine these criteria and the achievements of award winners.

Academic libraries, even when they have not explicitly adopted a quality management approach, have often used particular techniques taken from this school of management practice. For example there has been considerable interest in *benchmarking* between academic libraries as a means of checking performance and finding useful ideas from other libraries. This is described in the next chapter.

Conclusion

Good management is crucial to the effectiveness and efficiency of the library and to the achievement of its long-term aims. Managers provide vision and leadership, allocate resources and are involved in decision making at every level of the organization. At present, managers are particularly involved in the management of change as libraries attempt to come to terms with new technological and learning environments, and it is to be expected that this requirement will continue.

In order to manage effectively it is important that good information is available, and considerable work has taken place to identify performance indicators which can aid decision making. Concern with provision of the highest standards of service have led to considerable interest in the techniques of quality management, which can provide a framework for the effective management of the library.

References

Brophy, P. (1991) The Mission of the Academic Library, *British Journal of Academic Librarianship*, **6** (3), 135-47.

Brophy, P. and Coulling, K. R. (1996) *Quality Management for Information and Library Managers*, Gower.

Corrall, S. (1994) *Strategic Planning for Library and Information Services*, Aslib.

European Foundation for Quality Management (2004) *Excellence Model* www.efqm.org/model_awards/model/excellence_model.htm.

Pedler, M., Burgoyne, J. and Boydell, T. (1991) *The Learning Company: a strategy for sustainable development*, McGraw-Hill.

Further reading

Pantry, S. and Griffiths, P. (2000) *Developing a Successful Service Plan*, Library Association Publishing.

Allan, B. (2004) *Project Management: tools and techniques for today's information professional*, Facet Publishing.

13
Performance measurement

Introduction

The measurement of the performance of processes and systems goes back at least as far as the invention of manufacturing technologies at the start of the Industrial Revolution – indeed it could be argued that it goes back to the earliest human societies, where no doubt the performance of individual hunter-gatherers was watched closely by the group! However, systematic approaches are most usefully traced to the development and acceptance of Frederick W. Taylor's management theories (and specifically the 1909 publication of his *Principles of Scientific Management*), which led to an emphasis on inspection and control. Although he built on the work of earlier theoreticians and practitioners, it was Taylor's emphasis on practical application, and on the need for managers to design work, that led to widespread acceptance of his methods. He was able to point to considerable successes in the ways he employed his theories. For example, he systematically examined the process of shovelling coal at the Bethlehem steelworks and was able to redesign the shovels used for each grade. As a result the workforce of 'coal shovellers' was cut from 500 to 140. Other managers and owners were quick to take notice of his revolutionary methods and to apply them to their own industries. It was only gradually that the limitations of this highly mechanistic approach, which in effect treated human beings as machines, came to be recognized.

In 1931 – the same year that Ranganathan's 'Laws' appeared (see Chapter 3) – W. A. Shewhart published *Economic Control of Quality of Manufactured Products* (Shewhart, 1931). This contribution marked a shift towards the use of statistical methods, and from these beginnings statistical quality control developed. While the emphasis still remained on the productivity of the individual worker, more attention started to be paid to scientific approaches to management. A number of different schools of thought developed, most notably operational (or operations) research which encouraged the formation of multi-disciplinary teams to bring a range of techniques to bear on complex organizational problems. Linear, and later dynamic, programming was introduced to enable complex management and organizational problems to be tackled. For a time, organization & methods (O&M) and work study became fashionable.

More recently, human relations approaches have become more prominent, recognizing that full participation by all employees, in decision making as well as in production, produces significant benefits. Currently the emphasis is on holistic approaches which involve a focus on benefits as well as costs and on the interests of all stakeholders, both internal and external. However, running through all of these approaches are two threads: an enduring search for 'quality', which we considered above, and a need for robust and rigorous performance indicators. The nature of these indicators can be seen to mirror the dominant management theories of the day. Libraries have followed these trends closely.

Library performance

Determining whether a library is providing a good service has occupied the attention of practitioners and researchers for many years. In the 1960s and 1970s a series of research studies were carried out, at that time naturally focusing on traditional library services, linked to the dominant management theories of the time as outlined above. Many of these contributions are well worth reading even in the context of electronic and hybrid services. For example, Orr (1973) explored what we mean by 'goodness' in the context of library services while Morse (1968) looked at 'library effectiveness'.

More recently, some of the most influential work has been undertaken in the USA by Nancy Van House, Charles R. McClure and their colleagues (e.g. Van House, Weil and McClure, 1990; McClure and Lopata, 1996) and in the UK under the influence of SCONUL. There have also been a number of projects and initiatives in this area. A particularly important publication was produced in 1995 under the title of *The Effective Academic Library* (Higher Education Funding Council for England, 1995), and set out a five-fold model for the assessment of effectiveness. The work was undertaken in response to a recommendation of the Follett Report that a framework of coherent and generic performance indicators, suitable for assessing academic libraries, should be established. The ensuing report provided a framework of factors to be considered:

- *integration*: the level of integration between the mission, aims and objectives of the institution and those of the library (5 indicators)
- *user satisfaction*: surveys and other feedback (e.g. course review, suggestions) (5 indicators)
- *delivery*: are stated objectives being met and is the volume of outputs high? (7 indicators)
- *efficiency*: outputs related to resource input (9 indicators)
- *economy*: cost per student (7 indicators).

The work tried to take into account the very different missions being pursued by institutions across the sector. So, under 'delivery', the questions addressed are whether the library is meeting *its own* objectives. These may relate to archival, research-oriented collections or to undergraduate textbook collections, and clearly the indicators of performance will be very different (see also the discussion in Chapter 8). This was a welcome shift from some earlier approaches, which judged all academic libraries by the same yardstick.

Work on performance indicators has also taken place in the European context and internationally under the aegis of both the International Federation of Library Associations and Institutions (IFLA) and the International Organization for Standardization (ISO). The latter has published International Standard 11620 (ISO, 1999) which contains indicators on which international agreement has been reached.

It is worth noting at this point that great care is needed when interpreting performance indicators, and it should be stressed that the reason that the term 'performance indicator' is generally preferred to 'performance measure' is that interpretation is always necessary. The figures produced are indicative of a situation which may need to be investigated or monitored.

The need for careful interpretation of performance indicators can be illustrated by some simple examples. Many reports on academic libraries use total expenditure as an indicator of performance, with the unwritten assumption that high levels of expenditure indicate a good library service.

But of course everything depends on how well the funding is spent. A relatively poorly funded library which is highly successful in targeting its expenditure towards user needs may be providing a better service than its more generously funded counterpart. A library with high levels of user visits may simply be failing to deliver adequate services to the users' workstations, so forcing them to pay a visit to the library building instead of accessing the equivalent service electronically. A library with high levels of enquiries might be struggling to cope with students who have received little or no information skills training. One area where there should be little room for interpretation or excuses is in user satisfaction, although even here subtle factors can be at work such as low expectations leading to high satisfaction with mediocre services – but that discussion is beyond the scope of this book.

Statistics

Academic libraries have collected comprehensive statistics on their operations for many years. The collection is co-ordinated by SCONUL (see Chapter 14) with the processing of the data undertaken by the Library & Information Statistics Unit (LISU) at Loughborough University. The annual statistics are published together with trend analysis and a commentary by LISU. For example, in 2003 LISU reported:

> Over the sector as a whole, library expenditure has kept pace with both general inflation and the increases in student numbers over the last five years. Academic libraries spent £447 million in 2001-02, £282 per FTE student. Spending was highest in the old universities at £347 per student (slightly lower than last year), and lowest in the new universities at £217. HE colleges spent an average of £223 per FTE student, an increase of 4.2% over the previous year.
>
> (LISU, 2003)

These statistics are important for a number of purposes. Firstly they help in the management of the local library, by drawing attention to local changes. So for example, the librarian needs to know if issue figures are falling or entrance counts rising in order to plan staffing needs. Secondly they are important when aggregated so that the overall development of the academic library sector can be assessed – such statistics were important in the Follett Committee's deliberations, to give one example, and helped make the case to government for funding. Used judiciously statistics can be persuasive; conversely the lack of statistical evidence may rouse suspicion or lead to an argument being dismissed for lack of evidence. Thirdly, statistics are important for accountability, so that libraries can demonstrate what they have produced for the resources invested in them. Finally, academic library statistics may contribute to national issues of strategic importance, as in 2004 during the debate in the House of Commons on scholarly communication when the cost to universities of purchasing academic journals was highlighted.

Methods for measuring performance

Although now somewhat dated, and having been overtaken by developments in electronic services, the classic *Academic Library Performance: a practical approach* (Van House, Weil and McClure, 1990) remains an important contribution, setting out the basic principles of performance measurement for academic libraries. The American researchers' aim in the first of these studies was to present a set of practical output measures for academic and research libraries. The measures were deliberately service-oriented and, as such, were not concerned with a library's internal functions, such as speed of processing new acquisitions, which support service but do not provide it directly. Emphasis was given to the design of surveys to inform measures concerned with issues such as general user satisfaction, satisfaction with reference services and so on.

As with most methods for measuring library performance the underlying model is what is known as the 'general systems model'. This recognizes that organizations operate in a broader environment, from which they draw resources and which they affect in terms of their outputs. Figure 13.1 illustrates this in its simplest form.

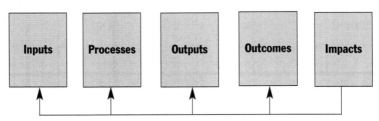

Figure 13.1 The General Systems Model

The *inputs* which are received, in the context of an academic library, may be revenue and capital budgets, staffing, the building itself and other services supplied by the institution. The library applies *processes* to these inputs - cataloguing and classification would be good examples - to produce *outputs*, such as catalogued and classified books on the library shelves. These outputs produce *outcomes*, for example when a user photocopies a chapter of a book or reads a journal article acquired from the library. At the end of the chain are *impacts*, which occur when a user is changed in some way: he or she may become more knowledgeable, for example, and that new knowledge may lead to a new invention. Clearly it is at the impact stage that the library is having most effect, and it is legitimate to ask how specific impacts can be encouraged. The following list illustrates some of the possible impacts that a library might want to achieve under different headings (adapted from Brophy, 2002):

- Learning
  - Increased literacy of users.
  - Students passing formal assessments and gaining their degrees.
- The library building
  - An architectural statement which draws attention to the social and cultural values of the university.
  - Happy users, made so by a comfortable environment which is warm, quiet, with nice chairs, a coffee bar, etc.
- Archive
  - Objects still available, in good condition, in 100 years' time.
  - Recognition as a resource of national importance through exposure on prime time TV documentaries on historical subjects.
- Provision of access to the world's recorded knowledge
  - All requested information is always immediately available, so users are never frustrated in their information access.
  - Unknown sources are brought to customers' attention so that they become informed without having to first make a request.
  - Facilities and services universally available, so that every member of the institution has, and uses, access.
- Filtering of information
  - Users do not suffer from information overload and are therefore less stressed than in the average university!

Measuring performance in networked environments

Over the last few years there has been considerable interest in developing performance indicators for the electronic library. There have been a number of strands of work in this area. One, in the USA, centred on research at Syracuse University and more recently at the State University of New York at Albany and Florida State University. The ARL emetrics project is described by Blixrud and Kyrillidou (2003), who provide a chronology of American activity in this field, illustrating that statistics on electronic services have been collected for many years. What is new is the attempt to devise robust performance indicators from this wealth of data.

Another strand of research and development, this time in the UK at the Centre for Research in Library and Information Management (CERLIM) at the Manchester Metropolitan University, included a study for the eLib Programme (Brophy and Wynne, 1998) and a major European Commission-funded project, EQUINOX. The EQUINOX work was closely related to the ISO standard 11620 (*Information and documentation: library performance indicators*) and was instrumental in the extension of that standard to include electronic library performance indicators.

Further UK work in this field has been undertaken by the University of Central England in the eVALUEd project, which has produced a toolkit for qualitative evaluation (as opposed to the mainly quantitative approaches used so far) of electronic information and library services (Thebridge, 2004).

Project COUNTER is a particularly interesting example of collaborative work in this field. It emerged from the identification of a common problem with data on the use of dataservices, namely that it was difficult to be sure that services were actually measuring and reporting the same thing. One service might, for example, report a 'use' on the basis of a query processed. Another might interpret 'use' as the delivery of information content, and so on. COUNTER has published a code of practice, showing, for example, exactly how a report entitled 'number of successful full-text article requests by month and journal' should be derived, structured and presented. Uniform reporting not only assists management directly but enables individual vendors' reports to be processed and amalgamated automatically.

Work on electronic library performance indicators is continuing, but will clearly be important in enabling managers to assess the performance of both electronic and hybrid services, and thus to manage their deployment and development.

Measuring service quality

There are a number of different approaches to measuring service quality, the simplest of which rely on straightforward customer satisfaction surveys. Bearing in mind that quality can only be defined in terms of customer needs, this is an entirely appropriate way to gain an overall view of quality. However, many librarians have realized that in order to be useful in terms of managing services, the quality and satisfaction models need to be broken down into their different component concepts.

LibQUAL+™ consists of a set of methodologies and instruments based upon the SERVQUAL methodology developed by Parasuraman, Zeithaml and Berry (1985). The essence of this approach lies in measuring the differences or 'gaps' between users' *expectations* of a service and their actual *experience* of using it. An additional set of questions can be used to determine the *desirable* level of service, i.e. what the users would like in an ideal (or at least better!) world. Pioneered by the Association of Research Libraries (ARL) in the USA, in partnership with Texas A&M University, LibQUAL+ has been widely used in North America while SCONUL has implemented a pilot and extended trials in the UK. The methodology has been described by Cook (2001).

Blixrud (2002) reports that over 78,000 individuals were surveyed by LibQUAL+ partners during 2002, producing initial findings that the dimensions of service that make up a library user's perception of service quality include:

- Service affect; i.e. responsiveness, assurance, empathy, and reliability – the human dimensions of library service
- Library as place; i.e. the campus as a centre of intellectual life, but this may not be a concern if other physical facilities are adequate
- Personal control; i.e. ability to navigate both the information universe in general and the web in particular
- Information access; i.e. ubiquity of access meaning information delivered in the format, location, and time of choice and comprehensive collections.

These dimensions form the basis for the 22 core questions used in surveying library users. From the answers to these questions it is possible to determine any areas of operation where experience falls short of expectations; in some cases it may also reveal that the library is delivering beyond expectations and even beyond what is deemed desirable.

Benchmarking

The idea behind benchmarking is to formalize comparisons with other organizations which have something in common with one's own. Benchmarking is concerned with developing systematic and structured approaches to finding and implementing best practice. It links the identification of the best way of doing things in the sector (or even outwith the sector if useful examples can be found) with a determination to improve one's own organization and 'to be the best'.

Benchmarking can be internal or external. That is, it can be done within the library, maybe across divisions or sections or maybe just by comparing new and old ways of doing things. Or it can be done externally, by comparing the library with others. Some sectors, including libraries in some countries, have developed their own 'benchmarking clubs', where organizations agree to work together to share benchmarking methods and data. In the UK SCONUL has supported some pilot benchmarking and produced a *Benchmarking Manual* which used a seven stage model: Defining; Partnering; Agreeing; Measuring; Collecting; Analysing; Acting.

While benchmarking may be more or less formal, it is often associated with iterative processes that draw in a range of both quantitative and qualitative methodologies. Rather than focusing on a particular technique or on the whole organization, it seeks to use appropriate methodologies to explore particular issues in depth – before moving on to the next issue. It therefore encourages managers to range across the available techniques to select those which best suit a particular purpose, to undertake that analysis, determine and implement action, review – and move on.

There is now considerable experience of benchmarking in the library sector. Creaser (2003) notes that the following benefits were observed from one academic library benchmarking exercise in the UK:

- Establishment of best practice
- Process improvements (large and small)
- Continued evaluation of customer opinion and needs
- Identification and validation of clear trends
- Networking between groups of staff involved in similar operations (quoted by many as 'invaluable')
- Exchange of views (and the generation of new ideas!)
- Staff development including learning new analysis methods such as process improvements and activity based costing (ABC)
- Greater local ownership of processes and tasks
- Changing perspectives about individual roles and also overall purpose (both for library and for academic staff and students)
- University recognition by establishing a solid reputation for the active use and implementation of benchmarking performance measurement methods.

The Balanced Scorecard

The Balanced Scorecard is in essence a way of grouping performance indicators so that an overall and balanced view of the organization can be obtained. It derives from the work of Kaplan and Norton (1992) in the USA but has been developed for use in the library sector by Poll in Germany (Poll, 2001) among others. In the USA the Library of Congress even has a video presentation available (see www.loc.gov/flicc/video/balance/balancedscore.html). As Poll remarks, 'service quality has many aspects - the Balanced Scorecard attempts to integrate them'.

The particular value of the Balanced Scorecard is that it ensures that the library is assessed from a range of different standpoints: that of the user; that of resource utilization; that of internal processes; and that of learning and growth of the organization. These four perspectives are centred around clarity of vision, of values and of strategy. In the Balanced Scorecard methodology, there is particular emphasis on the 'double feedback loop'. This means that not only does feedback relate to the organization's outputs, but it also relates to the outcomes and impacts.

The Balanced Scorecard helps an organization to check whether improvements in one area may have been achieved at the expense of another, and so keeps the whole organization in balance. Its underlying philosophy is very different to that of earlier control-based systems. As Kaplan and Norton (1992) noted:

> . . . because traditional measurement systems have sprung from the finance function, the systems have a control bias. That is, traditional performance measurement systems specify the particular actions they want employees to take and then measure to see whether the employees have in fact taken those actions. In that way, the systems try to control behaviour. Such measurement systems fit with the engineering mentality of the Industrial Age. The Balanced Scorecard, on the other hand . . . puts strategy and vision, not control, at the centre. It establishes goals but assumes that people will adopt whatever behaviour and take whatever actions are necessary to arrive at those goals.

In some quarters the Balanced Scorecard is seen as a reaction to benchmarking, which can have the disadvantage of fixing attention on a limited number of aspects of a library's operation. The Balanced Scorecard is useful for countering any such tendency.

Conclusion

The assessment of the performance of an academic library is a complex topic. The techniques and models used have developed rapidly in recent years and now provide sophisticated mechanisms for assessing the outcomes, and to some extent the impacts, of the academic library. Perhaps we are now seeing a movement beyond individual techniques in an attempt to draw on the best of what is now many years' experience and to synthesize the different approaches. As this becomes more commonplace, we will undoubtedly find ourselves looking closely at the question of impact. Do our libraries actually do any good? If we can demonstrate that they do, we will win many of the critical arguments which will affect their future.

References

Blixrud, J. C. (2002) Evaluating Library Service Quality: use of LibQUAL+™. *IATUL Proceedings (new series) 12, 23rd Annual IATUL Meeting, June 2-6, 2002, Kansas City, KS, USA.*

Blixrud, J. C. and Kyrillidou, M. (2003) E-Metrics: next steps for measuring electronic resources, *ARL*, 230/231 (October/December), 11-13, www.arl.org/newsltr/230/emetrics.html.

Brophy, P. (2002) The Evaluation of Public Library Online Services: measuring impact, MLA,
www.peoplesnetwork.gov.uk/documents/impact-issue-paper.pdf.

Brophy, P. and Wynne, P. M. (1998) *Management Information Systems and Performance Measurement for the Electronic Library: final report*, LITC, www.ukoln.ac.uk/dlis/models/studies/mis/mis.doc.

Cook, C. (ed.) (2001) The Maturation of Assessment in Academic Libraries: the role of LibQUAL+™, *Performance Measurement and Metrics*, **3** (2), 34-112.

Creaser, C. (ed.) (2003) *As Other See Us: benchmarking in practice*, LISU Occasional Paper No. 33, LISU, www.lboro.ac.uk/departments/dis/lisu/downloads/OP33.pdf.

Higher Education Funding Council for England (1995) *The Effective Academic Library: a framework for evaluating the performance of UK academic libraries: a consultative report to HEFC(E), SHEFC, HEFC(W) and DENI by the Joint Funding Council's Ad Hoc Group on performance indicators for libraries*, HEFC(E).

Kaplan, R. S. and Norton, D. P. (1992) The Balanced Scorecard: measures that drive performance, *Harvard Business Review*, (Jan-Feb), 71-9.

Library and Information Statistics Unit (2003) *LISU Annual statistics 2003*, www.lboro.ac.uk/departments/dils/lisu/downloads/als03exec.pdf.

McClure, C. R. and Lopata, C. I. (1996) *Assessing the Academic Networked Environment: strategies and options*, CNI Publications.

Morse, P. M. (1968) *Library Effectiveness: a systems approach*, MIT Press.

Orr, R. H. (1973) Measuring the Goodness of Library Services: a general framework for considering quantitative measures, *Journal of Documentation*, **29** (3), 313-32.

Parasuraman, A., Zeithaml, V. A. and Berry, L. L. (1985) A Conceptual Model of Service Quality and its Implications for Future Research, *Journal of Marketing*, **49** (4), 41-50.

Poll, R. (2001) Performance, Processes and Costs: managing service quality with the Balanced Scorecard, *Library Trends*, **49** (4), 709-17.

Shewhart, W. A. (1931) *Economic Control of Quality of Manufactured Product*, Macmillan.

Taylor, F. W. (1909) *Principles of Scientific Management*, Harper Bros.

Thebridge, S. (2004) The eVALUEd Toolkit: practical evaluation help for academic libraries, *Performance Measurement and Metrics*, 5 (2), 72–80.

Van House, N. A., Weil, B. T. and McClure, C. E. (1990) *Measuring Academic Library Performance: a practical approach*, American Library Association.

Further reading

EQUINOX
   http://equinox.dcu.ie/
eVALUEd Toolkit
   www.evalued.uce.ac.uk/about.htm
LibQUAL+™
   www.libqual.org
Library and Information Statistics Unit (LISU)
   www.lboro.ac.uk/departments/dils/lisu/index.html
Project COUNTER
   www.projectcounter.org/

14
Professional issues

Introduction

As professionals, academic librarians have obligations which derive from their professional status, just as much as any other professional grouping. Indeed, the whole point of a 'profession' is not, as George Bernard Shaw suggested, 'a conspiracy against the laity' but rather the acceptance of obligations to one's clients which transcend the purely legal and bureaucratic and which acknowledge that their interests must be protected. A professional is not simply an employee or interested solely in profit and personal advantage: the award and achievement of professional status carries with it the assumption that the professional accepts responsibilities to his or her clients. Indeed the use of terminology such as 'client' can be an important signal that the person being served is more than a mere 'customer' and that the relationship is more than that of mutual self-interest.

Because librarians are information and knowledge workers, their professional obligations focus on access to and the use of information. In this chapter we consider the major issues which this raises.

Professional conduct

Librarians in the UK have a code of professional conduct, published by the Chartered Institute of Library and Information Professionals (which is described later in this chapter) and based on the following principles:

> The conduct of members should be characterised by the following general principles, presented here in no particular order of priority:

1   Concern for the public good in all professional matters, including respect for diversity within society, and the promoting of equal opportunities and human rights.
2   Concern for the good reputation of the information profession.
3   Commitment to the defence, and the advancement, of access to information, ideas and works of the imagination.
4   Provision of the best possible service within available resources.
5   Concern for balancing the needs of actual and potential users and the reasonable demands of employers.
6   Equitable treatment of all information users.
7   Impartiality, and avoidance of inappropriate bias, in acquiring and evaluating information and in mediating it to other information users.
8   Respect for confidentiality and privacy in dealing with information users.
9   Concern for the conservation and preservation of our information heritage in all formats.
10 Respect for, and understanding of, the integrity of information items and for the intellectual effort of those who created them.
11 Commitment to maintaining and improving personal professional knowledge, skills and competences.
12 Respect for the skills and competences of all others, whether information professionals or information users, employers or colleagues.

(CILIP, 2004a)

The purpose of this framework is to assist professional librarians, in whatever sector they find themselves, to act ethically. The ethical principles are supported by a Code of Professional Practice which sets out personal responsibilities, responsibilities to information and its users, responsibilities to colleagues and the information community and responsibilities to society.

Professional associations
SCONUL

The Standing Conference of National and University Libraries (SCONUL) was founded in 1950 and in 1994 merged with the Council of Polytechnic Librarians, retaining its former name. In 2001 SCONUL changed its name to the Society of College, National and University Libraries, retaining its former acronym, when colleges of higher education were admitted to membership. Its members include virtually all the university and national libraries in the UK and the Republic of Ireland, represented usually by the university librarian or a member of staff of equivalent seniority. SCONUL meets formally twice a year but much of its work is done either by its secretariat in London or by its advisory committees, task forces and working parties. It serves as a forum for debate for senior academic librarians and has an important role as a representative body, maintaining close contacts with government departments and bodies which are influential in its field of interest.

The following are typical of the major issues considered by SCONUL in recent years:

- Intellectual property rights, including the EC Copyright Directive
- The 2004 Legal Deposit Libraries Bill, which provided for deposit of electronic publications
- Quality assurance in academic libraries, including involvement with the LibQUAL+ methodology described in Chapter 13
- The House of Commons enquiry into scholarly communication, including the role of institutional repositories
- Relationships with publishers and with the Copyright Licensing Agency, especially in relation to electronic publishing
- Access to libraries by users with disabilities, including the implications of SENDA
- The RSLG and the establishment of the Research Libraries Network (see Chapter 2)
- Piloting, in conjunction with the Open University, a module on information skills for first year undergraduate students.

SCONUL also collects a comprehensive set of statistical data from its members each year and publishes it in conjunction with the Library and Information Statistics Unit (LISU) at Loughborough University, as described in Chapter 13.

The Chartered Institute of Library and Information Professionals

The Library Association (LA) was founded in 1877 to unite 'all persons engaged or interested in library work for the purpose of promoting the best possible administration of libraries and the formation of new ones where desirable'. Its membership was drawn largely from the public libraries and during its early decades it was fairly ineffective, failing to attract into membership many librarians below the 'chief' level and not even many of those. The Association's University and Research Section was formed in 1928, but for many years attracted only a small proportion of those working in the academic sector.

One of the key achievements of The Library Association was the establishment of professional examinations leading to the status of chartered librarian. Although the tension between academic and professional qualifications has always been apparent in academic libraries, the status of chartered librarian became important in the sector only with the foundation of the new universities in the 1960s. However, by the end of that decade undergraduate and postgraduate courses in librarianship had become widespread and the Association's influence was then brought to bear through its course approvals procedures.

In 1958 a separate professional association, the Institute of Information Scientists (IIS), was set up by information professionals working mainly in the industrial and commercial sectors. The Institute placed emphasis on information storage and retrieval rather than on the library and attracted many members who were disenchanted by the perceived emphasis of the LA on public library affairs. Members were recruited in university libraries, particularly among those engaged in the provision of scientific and technical information and among subject librarians in those fields. Over the years, the IIS developed strong special interest groups (SIGs), of which the UK Online Users Group (UKOLUG) was the best known.

During 1998-2000 the IIS and the LA engaged in detailed discussions on a possible merger with the intention of forming a new professional body for the UK information profession. Agreement was reached and in April 2002 the Chartered Institute of Library and Information Professionals (CILIP) came into being.

CILIP states its mission as to:

- set, maintain, monitor and promote standards of excellence in the creation, management, exploitation and sharing of information and knowledge resources;

- support the principle of equality of access to information, ideas and works of the imagination which it affirms is fundamental to a thriving economy, democracy, culture and civilisation;
- enable its Members to achieve and maintain the highest professional standards in all aspects of delivering an information service, both for the professional and the public good. (CILIP, 2004b)

Of particular interest to academic librarians are the Special Interest Groups covering the field, the main ones being the University, College and Research Group with its journal *Relay* and the Colleges of Further and Higher Education Group which publishes *CoFHE Bulletin*.

Open access and the issue of censorship

At the heart of the library profession lies a belief that all citizens should have access to all legitimately open information. Although sometimes stated as 'everyone should have access to all information', this is clearly a nonsense. Some information – such as an individual's private papers or a company's legitimate trade secrets – is quite properly restricted. Where the dividing line should be drawn is a matter for debate, and that debate is sharpest when publicly produced information – i.e. information produced by or on behalf of public sector institutions – is at issue.

In the UK, after many years of debate, a Freedom of Information Act came fully into force on 1st January 2005 although some provisions had been in place since the Act was passed in 2000. It applies to all requests for information from a public body, including universities and colleges. However, it is not the only relevant legislation, since cognizance has also to be taken of the Environmental Information Regulations and sundry other statutes and regulations. Most higher and further education institutions have centralized mechanisms in place to deal with requests under these provisions, and it is important that these departments be consulted if formal requests are received from internal or external customers.

It is worth remembering that there is never wholly open access to all information. Even where it is accepted that, as a matter of principle, information should be open and accessible, societies always place some restrictions on information availability. One example is that it is generally felt undesirable for children to be exposed to scenes of explicit sex and violence, and the film and video certification procedures – to give a case in point – have been developed to achieve this. Such actions would not normally be regarded as censorship nor would they contravene the open access legislation. In academic institutions, however, such restrictions would hardly ever apply, as a recent case makes clear. The West Midlands Police Paedophile and Pornography Squad confiscated a copy of Robert Mapplethorpe's work from the library of the University of Central England (UCE). A third-year student in the Birmingham Institute of Art and Design intended to use photographs of images from the book in a piece of coursework entitled 'Fine Art versus Pornography'. The film was taken to a local chemist for developing and the chemist forwarded the negatives to the police, who passed the book and papers in the case to the Crown Prosecution Service on the basis that the book contravened the Obscene Publications Act. The University stood firm on the issue of freedom of academic enquiry, and eventually the CPS decided not to pursue the case (University of Central England, 2000).

Confidentiality, privacy and data protection

It is generally accepted in Western societies, though not necessarily in others, that individuals have a right to privacy – this right is enshrined in Article 8 of the European Convention on Human Rights. Some countries have laws to guard against media intrusion into the private lives of individuals, although the UK does not.

In the past privacy considerations have not been a major issue for academic libraries, since there was relatively little information of a private nature which they held, although an exception to this would be information on books or other items borrowed by individuals. It is generally accepted that libraries should not disclose such information to third parties, and in higher education this should be taken to include a student's tutor.

With the development of electronic systems, the opportunities for breaching an individual's privacy have multiplied. As long ago as 1984 the UK introduced its first *data protection* legislation, which placed requirements on organizations to take steps to ensure that data held electronically was limited and protected. The 1984 legislation laid down eight principles:

- Data must only be obtained fairly and legally.
- It can only be held for purposes declared by the organization.
- It can only be used or disclosed to others in accordance with the organization's declaration.
- It must be limited to data which is adequate for, relevant to and not excessive for the declared purposes.
- It must be accurate and must be kept up to date.
- It must not be kept longer than necessary.
- On request, the subject of the data must be provided with a copy.
- There must be proper protection against unauthorized disclosure.

All data held in library computer systems which can be linked to individuals must be properly registered – this will usually be through the university's data protection officer. Data covered by the current legislation (in essence the Data Protection Act 1998) includes not only user registration and borrowing records, but catalogue records where an individual author is named.

The original 1984 legislation has been modified as a result of European Union directives and has recently been extended to include paper-based data, i.e. not only electronic records in computer systems.

Copyright

Copyright is the term used for the legal protection of publications and other 'original literary, dramatic, musical or artistic works . . . sound recordings, films, broadcasts and cable programmes', in the words of the 1988 Copyright, Designs and Patents Act. Copyright is one of a number of intellectual property rights (IPR) which include patents, trademarks, some classes of confidential information and industrial designs. Copyright is automatic and does not have to be claimed, although many publishers like to place a copyright statement on the verso of a book's title page.

In essence, a work which is copyright – and it is safest to assume that all library stock and all information objects accessed, including all web pages, are copyright unless they are known not to be – may be copied only with the rights holder's permission. There are however some exceptions to this. An individual may make a limited copy, although not by electronic means, under what is known as 'fair dealing' for the purpose of non-commercial research or private study – it should be noted that this excludes class use of copies. What is 'fair' is not defined in the legislation and would need to be assessed in each case. Thus, although it is sometimes said that one chapter out of a book would be a 'fair' amount to copy, this might not be the case if that one chapter contained the key research results, say, while the rest consisted of introductory material.

Academic libraries are 'prescribed libraries' for the purposes of the legislation, which enables them to provide a copying service for non-commercial purposes and to undertake copying for a number of purposes, such as preservation, which would not otherwise be allowed. There are also recent provisions to allow copying of material for people with visual impairments without seeking the copyright holders' permission, provided specific conditions are followed.

There are a number of licensing schemes in operation which enable copies to be made by members of higher education institutions if a licence is held. The most important of these is the scheme run by the Copyright Licensing Agency (CLA), which includes multiple copying for class use. There are also schemes for copying of slides, of television programmes and of various other materials. Where no licence is available or where the licence is not held it is essential that permission to copy is obtained from the rights holder.

Copyright and other intellectual property legislation is complex and cannot be described fully in a short section in a more general text. Reference should be made in the first instance to a standard text on the subject and to the copyright guides published by CILIP (see Cornish (2004a, 2004b); these also provide up-to-date information on changes to UK copyright legislation which have occurred as a result of European Union directives.

Plagiarism

The problem of plagiarism has become more pronounced since students started to make extensive use of electronic sources, although it has always been present. In essence plagiarism involves passing off another person's work as your own. While quoting from another person's work is perfectly acceptable and indeed is encouraged in academic writing, the source of the quotation must always be given and the amount of material used must not be excessive. Because it is so easy to find material on the web, students may be tempted to download relevant papers and then cut and paste sections into their essays. It can then be difficult to detect that the work is not their own.

The JISC has taken a lead in providing both advice to institutions (through a Plagiarism Advisory Service at the University of Northumbria) and, through that organization, making available a plagiarism detection service. There is concern in academic institutions that students' attitudes to plagiarism have changed, and that not everyone takes it as seriously as they should. The issue is set out in the following quotation:

> The learning objectives set for most assessments, most of which are now far more clearly communicated to students than may have been the case in the past, stress skills such as the selection, assembly and manipulation of information; using information in new ways, making new links and drawing new conclusions. None of this countenances the presenting of the words of others as if they were the student's own. This is still, explicitly and implicitly, recognised as a form of cheating.
>
> (Larkham, 2003)

Responsibilities to future generations

A final issue which may be considered under the heading of 'professional issues' is the way in which academic librarians discharge their responsibilities to future generations. In Chapter 4 we defined one of the academic library's stakeholders as 'Posterity – future users of materials which are currently being added to stock'. It is easy to forget, in an era when the predominant approach has shifted from holdings to access, that librarians need to consider how their present-day actions will impact on future users. The academic libraries which we have today are based on the decisions and actions of earlier generations of librarians and the collection strengths of present university libraries are a testament to the longer view that they took. Perhaps the most obvious area for concern is the lack of systematic preservation of the electronic record of human knowledge, an issue discussed in Chapter 8. However, a broader view of professional responsibilities might take in other issues as well: building design, research into library practice and professional education are examples of areas which ought to receive attention.

Conclusion

Librarians are professionals and must take their duty to their clients seriously. CILIP has provided guidance in the form of its *Code of Professional Practice*, and the professional associations are heavily involved in the accreditation of courses and the provision of continuing professional development. Many of the issues which concern academic librarians are of profound importance for society as a whole: freedom of information and censorship; confidentiality; privacy; data protection; copyright; and plagiarism. It is especially important that librarians consider carefully their responsibilities to future generations, since among their duties is that of helping to preserve the memory of humanity. Taken together, these issues present a considerable agenda of issues for the academic librarian.

References

Chartered Institute of Library and Information professionals (2004a) *Ethical Principles and Code of Professional Practice for Library and Information Professionals*, CILIP,
www.cilip.org.uk/professionalguidance/ethics/default.htm.

Chartered Institute of Library and Information professionals (2004b) *Mission Statement: what we stand for*, CILIP,
www.cilip.org.uk/aboutcilip/missionstatement

Cornish, G. P. (2004a) *Copyright: interpreting the law for libraries, archives and information services*, 4th edn, Facet Publishing.

Cornish, G. P. (2004b) *Guidelines on the Recent Changes to Copyright Law*, CILIP, www.cilip.org.uk/NR/rdonlyres/C0627F34-2D98-4BD3-9CCC-765D787D374E/0/mcglaca_legislationguidelines.pdf.

Larkham, P. J. (2003) Exploring and Dealing with Plagiarism: traditional approaches, http://online.northumbria.ac.uk/faculties/art/information_studies/Imri/Jiscpas/site/pubs_goodprac_larkham.asp.

University of Central England (2000) *After a Year Out on Loan Mapple-thorpe Book is Set to Return to Library Shelves*, University of Central England, www.uce.ac.uk/mapplethorpe/.

Further reading

Office of the Information Commissioner
www.informationcommissioner.gov.uk/

15
The academic library of the future

Introduction

Academic libraries experienced a period of rapid and profound change in the closing decades of the 20th century. Although information technology was the main driving force, other issues were highly significant, including the 'massification' of higher education and changes in society's attitudes to education. For the foreseeable future it is clear that the process of change will continue, even if it is not at present possible to discern all the drivers which will contribute to this process. In this chapter we consider some of the issues which are most likely to change the nature of the academic library and, in their extreme forms, perhaps even threaten its existence.

Technological change: information resources

The pace with which the world wide web has developed, becoming the delivery medium of choice within a few years of its invention, should serve as an example, and perhaps a warning, of the way in which a technological innovation can affect the delivery of library services. The ability of anyone with a low specification PC and an internet connection to publish their own material in a way that makes it accessible throughout the world is perhaps the most revolutionary aspect of the web. But that is not to say that other, just as revolutionary, technological innovations may not be just around the corner.

One of the possible areas of impact for libraries is the development of the electronic journal. As we have seen (Chapter 8), to date most electronic journals have essentially been electronic copies of paper-based journals –

few have been truly electronic products, taking advantage of all the possibilities of the medium. For example, as yet there are few multimedia electronic journals, despite the scope for incorporating still and moving images, sound clips and the like in content. There are a number of reasons for the relatively slow progress that has been made in this area, including the economics of parallel and electronic publishing, uncertainties over copyright protection, the complexities of electronic peer review processes and sheer conservatism. However, it is quite possible that a single event could trigger a major shift from print to electronic. For example a decisive break in the cycle discussed earlier whereby universities generate the IPR, effectively give it to publishers and then buy it back again. A parallel investment in institutional eprint repositories would provide the impetus for an enormous change in the material handled by libraries.

If the situation with regard to journals is uncertain, that for books could be equally unpredictable. A number of current technological innovations could threaten both textbooks and scholarly monographs. These include:

- the widespread acceptance of a standard for electronic books, enabling publishers to reach a worldwide audience through a single format
- the successful production, at economic cost, of 'electronic paper' which enables data to be displayed using reflective light (as normal paper) with the ability to refresh the display at will
- truly usable hand-held e-books, with excellent displays suitable for long-term viewing.

While it seems likely that popular fiction and the like will still be produced in hardback and paperback printed editions to satisfy a mass market, the academic market could be vulnerable to a major shift in emphasis. The academic library would have to adjust to this change quickly if it were to survive.

A further area of opportunity lies in the development of learning object repositories. To date libraries have not been particularly active in securing a share in these developments, which is surprising since many of the issues are similar to those of which librarians have much experience (for example in terms of resource description). The JISC is funding a national repository, the JORUM (www.jorum.ac.uk/), which is designed to encourage the re-purposing and re-use of materials developed in UK education. This is part of the wider Exchange for Learning (X4L) Programme which involves around 100 UK institutions. Academic libraries need to be much more prominent in this kind of development.

Technological change: delivery systems

As available bandwidth in the home improves and as more and more services become accessible in this way, it is possible that a rapid change in library users' habits could occur. The home PC and television are in effect becoming the home information and communications centre, with all kinds of information services available through them. Already it is clear that, as far as libraries are concerned, we have all become distance learners since electronic delivery allows virtually every user to access library resources from remote locations.

A second area of development is in enhanced functionality for computer games consoles. Bearing in mind that very many young students, and particularly male students, entering higher education will be expert computer games players with all the latest gadgetry, the impact of internet-enabled computer games consoles could be significant. Rather than looking to the PC as the workstation of choice, such students may prefer to combine interactive games with more serious information gathering. The question will be who is best placed to exploit the constraints and capabilities of such systems – and it may not be libraries.

The concept of the internet-enabled refrigerator seems at first sight rather bizarre. However, the idea behind this kind of development is that home-based systems should be able to re-order supplies automatically for delivery by a supermarket when stocks run low, perhaps also running automatic checks to compare prices before deciding where to place the order. It is conceivable that the same principle could come into use for ordering information: for example, the required readings for course modules could be downloaded to students' homes automatically, or queries left on the system by a student in the evening could be used to secure the downloading of a mix of information sources during the following day, ready for the next evening's academic study.

A final example of technological change can be found in the rapid development of mobile communications. Web-based services are now routinely delivered across cellular and wireless networks to the user's temporary location. It is as yet too early to judge the impact of these developments, but librarians should not assume that the impact on their services will be either minimal or benign. To give an example, sections of this book were written on train journeys between north-west England and London, and the second edition was revised while travelling round Europe, with references checked online as needed. The convenience of being able to check those references across mobile or wireless (GPS, GPRS or WAP) connections – at reasonable cost – outweighed any perceived benefit of the alternative of a later, personal visit to the university library.

With the convergence of these kinds of technology, the future is very difficult to predict. While technology will undoubtedly open up many new possibilities for information delivery, other forces will also be at work. Not least it is important to remember that technologies of the kinds described above will not have universal market penetration for a long time, that many people will need the basic service of a place to study, and that existing systems and information collections (known as 'legacy systems') have enormous value locked up in them.

Virtual learning environments and the virtual university

Almost every university and college now operates a virtual learning environment (VLE). There is also a great deal of discussion of the 'virtual university' in higher education circles, with every institution examining the possibilities and pitfalls of delivering courses online and remotely. The examples most often quoted are from the USA, where the University of Phoenix in particular has been highly successful in recruiting students to its courses and in gaining formal accreditation. It is noticeable that the students enrolling on such courses are in the main professionals, people who are well motivated towards learning and in many cases people who are already juggling work, family and other responsibilities. In the UK, the situation is somewhat different to that in most countries because of the long-established Open University which has been offering distance learning at higher education level for nearly 40 years. Interestingly, the OU is shifting its emphasis somewhat, with less time spent on face-to-face tutoring and more on online equivalents. However, it should also be noted that an ambitious project to establish a UK e-university, which received funding of £62 million in 2001-2004, has proved unsuccessful and has been discontinued in favour of initiatives led by individual universities or consortia. Virtual approaches are important, but we have not yet found a dominant model.

Virtual learning environments which colleges and universities are putting in place typically feature:

- student guidance, enabling would-be students to assess the relevance of each course and module to their particular requirements
- a curriculum carefully constructed in manageable modules
- delivery using ICT-based techniques, with the emphasis shifting very much towards the role of the teacher as tutor
- online information resources, carefully organized within a consistent 'shell' so that students can become familiar with ways to access the resources, and including digitized lectures as well as more traditional 'published' resources
- systems to encourage and enable students to explore sources of information, but without imposing specific resources.
- online discussion, organized in a variety of ways including student–tutor, student–student and group work
- online assessment, including the use of both online submission of traditional assignments such as essays and reports and computer assessment, with automatic plagiarism detection
- management systems, to enable tutors to track students' progress and to support their work efficiently
- institutional audit systems, to ensure that students' progress is tracked and that their eligibility for exit awards, from certificates to degrees, is known
- careers advice systems, so that students can explore ways in which they can exploit their learning.

The attractions of moving to virtual operation are fairly obvious. In theory, there would be no need for expensive campuses, no need for student accommodation, no need for large library buildings, one member of staff could 'lecture' to unlimited numbers of students and the market would be world-wide. In practice there are several limitations which currently prevent such approaches becoming the norm, including the following:

1   The necessary technological infrastructure is lacking. Home ownership of PCs and broadband connections are not yet universal, so there are questions of how to serve disadvantaged groups.

2   The costs of developing online courses are very high, and can only be justified if large numbers of students can be recruited. This tends to lead to intense competition in a few areas (business, IT, etc.) and no provision in others (ancient history, minority cultures, etc.).

3   Teaching staff have not yet been trained to be effective and efficient in the virtual environment.

4   Tutor support systems are as yet inadequate. For example, tutors have to deal with a situation in which every enrolled student can potentially send them unlimited numbers of e-mails.

5   Student support systems are also inadequate. Libraries, for example, are very heavily used for the physical resources (textbooks, etc.) they provide, but provision to support virtual learners is very uneven.

6   Most learners do not like entirely online learning. This is perhaps the most fundamental issue of all. Is learning not in essence a social process, in which we learn by interacting with others? Is it possible or even desirable to replicate this in the virtual environment?

Many of these issues can be resolved - if they are to be resolved at all - only by taking a wider view and looking again at the place of education within society itself, with universities forging alliances with other educational providers to achieve the critical mass needed to make virtual or, more likely, hybrid learning systems feasible. The focus for much of this thinking is taking place under the banner of *lifelong learning*.

Lifelong learning

This topic was introduced in Chapter 1, but it is appropriate to return to it here. If we assume that government policies will be successful in attracting the majority of the population into continuous learning, the impacts on colleges and universities could be profound. As we move towards a situation where over half the adult population is graduate, a large proportion of lifelong learning needs will be postgraduate - updating knowledge and skills, conversion courses and so on. Taking the UK as an example, this implies that perhaps half of its 50 million population could be active postgraduate lifelong learners at any one time. This is not to say that they would all necessarily be taking course modules simultaneously, but they may all find it advantageous to be associated with an academic institution or at least with services such as the library. With around 200 major higher education providers in the UK, the average university will need to be providing a service to 100,000 students simultaneously, and many established universities could be looking at a student 'population' in excess of a quarter of a million.

The implications of this for academic libraries could be immense, bearing in mind the likelihood that many lifelong learners would find library access valuable even when not actively engaged in course work. How would they respond? Would they, for example, lose their focus on front-line services and become back-room technical services, crafting information resources to be selected by students and staff under self-service arrangements? Or would they become integrated parts of the delivery process? Just as interoperability between libraries and data services is one of the building blocks for hybrid library services, so interoperability between the elements of the learning environment and the library will be essential for the development of effective educational systems in the future. But does this imply an *educational* role for the academic library? As yet we do not know.

Globalization and regionalization

Whereas in the past libraries put together a local collection which was almost invariably dominated by the output of its own nation's publishers, even allowing for the increasing proportion of US imprints and for specialist collections, the globalization of trade and with it of information resources could have significant implications for libraries. The success of national publishing activity in global markets where there is less and less room for local products could determine which sources are available to libraries themselves and squeeze other sources out of the market. For example, there might be room for no more than one resource discovery service in each subject discipline and there is certainly no good reason for each library developing its own. In some subjects, particularly in the hard sciences, it is difficult to see the justification for proliferation, particularly if the local library can build localized services within its own portal using the international service as a major contributory source. In other subjects, such as law or cultural studies, global approaches will be far less appropriate but the costs of developing purely local solutions could be prohibitive. As a result subjects which can attract world-wide interest could benefit from the economies of scale that would result from libraries or other organizations across the world buying into a service, while those which are less popular or are culturally determined could struggle to attract adequate attention. This then raises the question for the local library as to how its role in redressing this balance should be interpreted.

One partial solution to the problems posed by globalization may be to form regional alliances. In the UK, which has for many years had a highly centralized government, there has been a recent policy shift towards greater devolution of power to regions. This is seen most obviously in the setting up of the Scottish Parliament and the Welsh Assembly, but it also affects the English regions. In terms of major library services, the UK has for many years presented a rather odd picture – the British Library, for example, has responsibilities across the UK, but there are national libraries of Scotland and Wales (but not of England or Northern Ireland, though of course there is the National Library of Ireland in Dublin in the Republic of Ireland). The Museums, Libraries and Archive Council has responsibility for England and to some extent for Wales but its remit does not extend to Scotland and Northern Ireland, although some of its activities do cover those countries – for example, in international representation.

Very many of the initiatives described in earlier chapters have had a national focus (eLib, RSLP, RLN, and so on) and some have deliberately linked libraries nationally in order to exploit joint strengths (CURL and Music Libraries Online would be obvious examples). A few (M25, NoWAL) have regional emphases. Achieving the right mix of local, regional, national, international and global co-operation and co-ordination will present a huge challenge and each academic library will need to position itself in this developing scenario.

Conclusion

Many of the above scenarios may appear to threaten the very existence of the academic library. It is all too easy, when faced with predictions of massive technology-led change, to assume that tomorrow's academic libraries will be little more than dehumanized gateways offering localized, and quite possibly impoverished, versions of groundbreaking, world-wide, multimedia information resource delivery systems, operated by major media conglomerates and delivered direct into students' and researchers' homes and laboratories. To draw such conclusions is, however, to forget that libraries have always been about far more than simple information access – they have never seen their role as purely putting books on shelves and leaving readers to find what they can.

First and foremost libraries are services. No service survives without continuously re-examining its products *and the ways in which they are delivered* to ensure that they meet their customers' real needs. It is worth returning to the discussion of quality management in Chapter 12, to recall that successful organizations the world over have put continuous improvement and customer satisfaction at the heart of their affairs. To take a customer-oriented view of the future academic library would be to place emphasis on user needs ahead of how those needs are met. It is inevitable that, in a book such as this, there will be a great deal of emphasis on the question of *how* services are provided. But to allow the 'how' to dominate the future would be to permit the means to dictate the ends.

In the final analysis, academic libraries are there to enable and enhance learning in all its forms – whether it be the learning of a first-year undergraduate coming to terms with what is meant by higher education or the learning of a Nobel Prize winning scientist seeking to push forward the frontiers of her discipline. In the Information Age it seems inconceivable that centres of information-handling expertise and guides to the ever-burgeoning information resources of the world will not be needed. By linking together higher education's objective of enabling learning for all who can benefit from it with their information-handling expertise, academic libraries should be able to create a vision of their future which is credible, attractive and attainable.

Further reading

Brophy, P. (2000) *The Library in the Twenty-first Century: new services for the information age*, Library Association Publishing.

Deegan, M. and Tanner, S. (2002) *Digital Futures: strategies for the information age*, Facet Publishing.

JISC X4L Programme
www.jisc.ac.uk/index.cfm?name=programme_x4l

Acronyms

AACR	Anglo-American Cataloguing Rules
ACN	Advisory Committee on Networking (see JCN)
ADAM	Art, Design, Architecture and Media Information Gateway (one of the original eLib subject gateways, but not funded as an RDN hub)
ADS	Archaeology Data Service
AFRC	Agriculture and Food Research Council
AHDS	Arts and Humanities Data Service
AHRC	Arts and Humanities Research Council (formerly Arts and Humanities Research Board)
ALA	American Library Association
APEL	Accreditation of Prior Experiential Learning
APL	Accreditation of Prior Learning
ARL	Association of Research Libraries (USA)
BBSRC	Biotechnology and Biological Sciences Research Council
BECTA	British Educational Communications and Technology Agency
BIDS	Bath Information and Data Services
BIOME	Health and life sciences hub (one of the RDN hubs)
BL	British Library
BLDSC	British Library Document Supply Centre
BLRDD	British Library Research and Development Department (responsibilities transferred to the LIC in 1998 and subsequently to MLA and AHRC)
BUFVC	British Universities Film and Video Council
BUILDER	Birmingham University Integrated Library Development and Electronic Resource (eLib project)
CAIRNS	Cooperative Academic Information Retrieval Network for Scotland (eLib project)

CALIM	Consortium of Academic Libraries in Manchester
CALT	Committee for Awareness, Liaison and Training (see JCALT)
CATS	Credit Accumulation and Transfer Scheme
CBL	Computer-Based Learning
CEDARS	CURL Exemplars in Digital Archives (eLib Project)
CEI	Committee on Electronic Information (see JCIIE)
CERLIM	Centre for Research in Library and Information Management (Manchester Metropolitan University)
CHEST	Combined Higher Education Software Team
CIE	Common Information Environment
CILIP	Chartered Institute of Library and Information Professionals
CIMI	Computer Interchange of Museum Information
CIT	Communications and Information Technologies (more usually ICT)
CMC	Computer-Mediated Communication
CNAA	Council for National Academic Awards
COPAC	CURL OPAC
CPD	Continuing Professional Development
CSCW	Computer Supported Collaborative Work
CSF	Critical Success Factor
CURL	Consortium of University Research Libraries
CVCP	Committee of Vice-Chancellors and Principals (now Universities UK)
CWIS	Campus Wide Information Service
DCMS	Department for Culture, Media and Sport
DDC	Dewey Decimal Classification
DENI	Department of Education Northern Ireland (acts as the funding council for Northern Ireland)
DfES	Department for Education and Skills
DISinHE	Disability Information Systems in Higher Education
DLI	Digital Libraries Initiative (USA)
DNER	Distributed National Electronic Resource (see also IE)
DSA	Disabled Student Allowance
DSC	see BLDSC
DTI	Department of Trade and Industry

EARL	Electronic Access to Resources in Libraries
EC	European Commission
ECDL	European Computer Driving Licence
EDDIS	Electronic Document Delivery – the Integrated Solution
EDI	Electronic Data Interchange
EDINA	Edinburgh Data and Information Access
EEVL	Edinburgh Engineering Virtual Library (one of the eLib subject gateways, now part of EMC)
EFQM	European Foundation for Quality Management
eLib	Electronic Libraries Programme
ELJ	Electronic Law Journals (eLib project)
EMC	Engineering, Mathematics and Computing hub (one of the RDN hubs)
EP	European Parliament
EPSRC	Engineering and Physical Resources Research Council
ERASMUS	European Community Action Scheme for the Mobility of University Students
ESF	European Social Fund
ESRC	Economic and Social Research Council
EU	European Union
FE	Further Education
FEFC	Further Education Funding Council
FIGIT	Follett Implementation Group for Information Technology
FOI	Freedom of Information
FTE	Full Time Equivalent
GILS	Government Information Locator Service
GIS	Geographic Information Systems
HDS	History Data Service
HE	Higher Education
HEA	Higher Education Academy
HEFC	Higher Education Funding Councils
HEFCE	Higher Education Funding Council for England
HEFCW	Higher Education Funding Council for Wales
HEI	Higher Education Institution
HEQC	Higher Education Quality Council
HERON	Higher Education Resources ON-Demand
HESA	Higher Education Statistics Agency

HESDA	Higher Education Staff Development Agency
HMI	Her Majesty's Inspectorate
HMSO	Her Majesty's Stationery Office
HNC	Higher National Certificate
HND	Higher National Diploma
HTML	HyperText Markup Language
HTTP	HyperText Transfer Protocol
Humbul	Humanities hub (one of the RDN hubs)
HyLiFe	Hybrid Library of the Future (eLib project)
IATUL	International Association of Technological University Libraries
ICT	Information and Communications Technologies
IFLA	International Federation of Library Associations and Institutions
IIP	Investors in People
ILEJ	Internet Library of Early Journals
ILL	Interlibrary Loan
ILTHE	Institute for Learning and Teaching in Higher Education (see HEA)
IP	Internet Protocol
IMPEL	Impact on People of Electronic Libraries (eLib study)
IMS	Instructional Management System
IPR	Intellectual Property Rights
ISAD(G)	General International Standard Archival Description
ISI	Institute for Scientific Information
ISO	International Organization for Standardization
ISP	Internet Service Provider
ISSC	Information Services Sub-Committee (former sub-committee of JISC)
ITT	Initial Teacher Training
JANET	Joint Academic Network
JCALT	JISC Committee for Awareness, Liaison and Training (formerly CALT)
JCCS	JISC Committee for Content Services
JCIIE	JISC Committee for the Integrated Information Environment (formerly JCIE, before that JCEI)
JCLT	JISC Committee for Learning and Teaching

JCN	JISC Committee on Networking (formerly the Advisory Committee on Networking)
JCSR	JISC Committee for the Support of Research
JISC	Joint Information Systems Committee
LAN	Local-Area Network
LASER	London and South East Region (library system)
LC	Library of Congress
LIC	Library and Information Commission (see MLAC)
LISU	Library and Information Statistics Unit
LLL	Lifelong Learning
LMS	Library Management System
LTSN	Learning and Teaching Support Network
MALIBU	Managing the hybrid Library for the Benefit of Users (eLib project)
MAN	Metropolitan Area Network
MARC	Machine Readable Cataloguing
MIA	MODELS Information Architecture
MIDAS	Manchester Information Datasets and Associated Services (now MIMAS, q.v.)
MIMAS	Manchester Information and Associated Services (see also MIDAS)
MIS	Management Information System
MLAC	Museums, Libraries and Archives Council
MLE	Managed Learning Environment
MODELS	MOving to Distributed Environments for Library Services (eLib project)
MRC	Medical Research Council
NAB	National Advisory Body
NCIP	North American Collection Inventory Project (USA)
NCT	National Co-ordination Team (of the TQEF)
NCVQ	National Council for Vocational Qualifications
NERC	Natural Environment Research Council
NESLI	National Electronic Site Licensing Initiative
NGfL	National Grid for Learning
NISS	National Information Services and Systems
NLB	National Library for the Blind
NLN	National Learning Network

NLS	National Library of Scotland
NLW	National Library of Wales
NoWAL	North West Academic Libraries
NREN	National Research and Education Network
NSF	National Science Foundation (USA)
NVQ	National Vocational Qualification
NWRLS	North West Regional Library System
OECD	Organization for Economic Cooperation and Development
OFSTED	Office for Standards in Education and Training
OLF	Open Learning Foundation
OMNI	Organizing Medical Network Information
OPAC	Online Public Access Catalogue
OTA	Oxford Text Archive
OU	Open University
PADS	Performing Arts Data Service
PCFC	Polytechnics and Colleges Funding Council
PFI	Private Finance Initiative
PI	Performance Indicator
PLN	Public Library Network
PRP	Performance-Related Pay
PSLI	Pilot Site Licence Initiative
PSIgate	Physical Sciences hub (one of the RDN hubs)
QA	Quality Assurance or Quality Assessment or Quality Audit
QAA	Quality Assurance Agency for Higher Education
RAE	Research Assessment Exercise
RDF	Resource Description Framework
RDN	Resource Discovery Network
RDNC	Resource Discovery Network Centre
RLG	Research Libraries Group (USA)
RNIB	Royal National Institute for the Blind
RNID	Royal National Institute for the Deaf
ROADS	Resource Organization And Discovery in Subject-based Services
RSLG	Research Support Libraries Group
RSLP	Research Support Libraries Programme
SCONUL	Society of College, National and University Libraries

SCRAN	Scottish Cultural Resources Access Network
SDI	Selective Dissemination of Information
SERC	Science and Engineering Research Council
SEREN	Sharing of Educational Resources in an Electronic Network
SET	Secure Electronic Transactions
SGML	Standard Generalized Markup Language
SHEFC	Scottish Higher Education Funding Council
SIG	Special Interest Group
SLA	Service Level Agreement
SME	Small and Medium-sized Enterprise
SOSIG	originally, Social Science Information Gateway, now Social sciences, business and law hub (one of the RDN hubs)
SPOT	Satellite Pour l'Observation de la Terre (MIMAS service)
SRHE	Society for Research in Higher Education
STV	Share The Vision
TASC	Technology Applications Sub-Committee (of JISC)
TEC	Training and Enterprise Council
THES	Times Higher Education Supplement
TLTP	Teaching and Learning Technology Programme
TQEF	Teaching Quality Enhancement Fund
TQM	Total Quality Management
UCAS	Universities and Colleges Admissions System
UCE	University of Central England
UCISA	Universities and Colleges Information Systems Association
UCL	University College London
UFC	Universities Funding Council
UfI	originally, University for Industry, now UfI (marketing its services as *learndirect*)
UGC	University Grants Committee
UKOLUG	UK Online Users Group (SIG of CILIP)
VADS	Visual Arts Data Service
VALNOW	Virtual Academic Library of the North-West (University of Central Lancashire)
VLE	Virtual Learning Environment
W3C	World Wide Web Consortium
WAB	Wales Advisory Board for Local Authority Higher Education

WAI	Web Accessibility Initiative (of W3C)
WAP	Wireless Application Protocol
WoPEc	Working Papers in Economics (eLib project)
WWW	World Wide Web
XML	eXtensible Markup Language
ZBB	Zero Base Budgeting

Index